D0387657

More Pages
from the *Red Suit* Diaries

# More Pages
# from the *Red Suit* Diaries

*A Real-Life Santa Shares Hopes,*
*Dreams, and Childlike Faith*

## Ed Butchart

Revell
*a division of Baker Publishing Group*
Grand Rapids, Michigan

Published by Revell
a division of Baker Publishing Group
P.O. Box 6287, Grand Rapids, MI 49516-6287
www.revellbooks.com

Printed in the United States of America

                Library of Congress Cataloging-in-Publication Data
Butchart, Ed.
    More pages from the red suit diaries : a real-life Santa shares
  hopes, dreams, and childlike faith / Ed Butchart.
      p.   cm.
    ISBN 978-0-8007-1904-3 (cloth)
    1. Santa Claus. 2. Department store Santas.  I. Title.
GT4985.B86  2008
394.2663—dc22                                    2008010296

In keeping with biblical principles of
creation stewardship, Baker Publishing Group advocates the responsible
use of our natural resources. As a
member of the Green Press Initiative,
our company uses recycled paper
when possible. The text paper of
this book is comprised of 30% post-
consumer waste.

green
press
INITIATIVE

To the God who loves me
and continues to bless me
far beyond my deserving

# Contents

*Dear Diary,*

There have been a lot of things that have influenced my life as Santa, but none has had a more profound and personal impact than the death of my Annie, my wonderful Mrs. Claus. It was the winter of 2004. She had been sick for a long time and had been in the ICU four times in our twenty-one years together. A couple of those times, her doctors told me there was nothing more they could do for her. But with hard praying— and her amazingly strong will to live—her health improved and she was allowed to come home again.

This time, however, was different. She told me she just couldn't pull off another miraculous recovery. She was simply too tired and weak to do it again. I begged her not to leave me. I told her I could not go on without her, and particularly could not go on being Santa. But she told me that I had to keep going. There were too many kids who believed in me, she said, and our love for Jesus demanded that I keep sharing that love with kids and adults. She told me not to mourn, because she knew where she was going and whom she would be with, and she wanted me to go on and be happy again. She slipped into a coma two days later and died on one of the most important days in our lives—Christmas.

The reaction of my family and friends was amazing. A good friend (and a fellow Santa) in High Point, North Carolina, sent me an email that said, "Boy, don't you know Annie had a glorious Christmas Day." My oldest son, Paul, responded, "That's great, Dad. Now you have something else to celebrate on Christmas: Annie's going home to heaven."

And that was so true. Annie was taken into the arms of Jesus, on the very day that we celebrate his birth. She was freed from all her pain, all the medications, and given a home in heaven on the day she and I had commemorated so many times in our Red Suits. We had always prayed that our portrayals would demonstrate God's love for his people. I know her love did just that.

# finding peace

## *Airbrake McGuirty*

For several summers I've been playing a character in a replica 1870s town—called Crossroads Village—at the Atlanta area's Stone Mountain Park, a historic theme park. My character is Airbrake McGuirty, a railroad engineer complete with requisite blue-and-white-striped overalls and hat. I was still grieving the loss of my Annie and found that going to Stone Mountain Park and becoming someone else for a few hours a day was good therapy. It helped me see that my life still had purpose.

Here's how Airbrake was born. In 2000 the management company at Stone Mountain Park opened the first element of Crossroads Village—a hamburger restaurant—with a grand opening scheduled for Memorial Day weekend. The theme of the restaurant was a diner for railroad crews, and the creators wanted a character to act as a host and entertainer—to greet customers and make them feel at home. They handed me a pair of striped overalls, a matching hat, and a work shirt and asked if I could create a character. I added a bandana, work gloves, and a pump oilcan with a long spout—the kind railroad men used to keep the steam locomotives running smoothly.

Nobody told me exactly what I should do other than "just entertain folks." When the ribbon was cut and the first customers arrived, I stood by the door and greeted them and helped them decipher the menu and place their orders. I tried to keep it light, bantering back and forth in my Airbrake persona. But it was only a few moments before my beard caught some visitors' attention. There was no way I could escape the Santa association. No matter how much I protested, I couldn't avoid it. So I decided to make it part of the fun.

I was carrying the oilcan around but couldn't figure out how to work it into my routine. When I spied the ketchup pump, inspiration hit me. I went into the kitchen, opened the oilcan, and poured it full of ketchup. I pumped it into the sink a few times to make sure it worked, then went back into the dining room.

I went up to a kid just about ready to bite into his hamburger and said, "How are the French fries?" Before he could reply, I said, "You need a little motor oil on them, don't you think?" Just as I started to pump, his mom yelped. When she saw it was just ketchup, she laughed. I knew I had found my gimmick. It was an easy way to divert attention away from my beard.

Unfortunately, I didn't wash out the can every night, and the acid in the tomatoes began to work on the metal parts of the pump. Soon the ketchup tasted terrible! So I put the gimmick aside for a few days. Then I found a homemade toy a friend had given me. He called it a "hooey stick." It was two pieces of wood of two different lengths. One was about a foot long and had a series of notches cut into its edges, with a small rectangular propeller attached at one end by a nail. The other piece of wood was about four inches long. The trick was to rub the small one along the notches on the big one and make the propeller turn. By skillful manipulation of the small stick, you could change the direction in which the propeller turned.

Kids and adults were amazed. They could not figure out how the contraption worked. To enhance the mystery, I would say the "secret word" just before the propeller reversed direction. The secret word was *hooey*. And when someone asked me how it worked, I'd reply, "It's just a bunch of hooey!" That silly gimmick has worked for more than four years now, and it has brought a lot of fun into people's lives, including my own.

I had a friend of mine produce five hundred hooey sticks. I packaged them in kits and sold them in Crossroads Village gift shops. Thanks to the generous management at the Park, all the proceeds went to my ministry, Friends of Disabled Adults and Children (FODAC). And anyone who bought one of the kits was entitled to one free hooey lesson from me.

More Pages from the Red Suit Diaries

## The Adventures of Airbrake

Being Airbrake was and is wonderful therapy for me. It gives me a chance to have in-depth visits with a lot of folks. I walk along the queues where the people are waiting to board the trains and talk to folks about where they're from and how they like the Park. Many people ask if I am Santa Claus. Most of the time I feign surprise that anyone would even make that connection. Then I add slyly, "Come back at Christmas and find out."

I do have a few ploys for avoiding direct questions about Santa, and most of the time it works. I tell people, "I'm not Santa; I'm the Easter Bunny!" Nobody believes that, of course, and I usually wind up whispering, "Shhh, don't tell anybody. I'm in disguise." That will usually work until they board the train and are pulling out of the station. Then there is a chorus of "Bye, Santa Claus!" from all the kids—and lots of the adults.

My primary job as Airbrake is to make the wait for the train seem shorter by entertaining with my hooey stick and engaging people in conversation. We host many international visitors, and it is always a treat to try to communicate with them. I do okay with Spanish, German, and American Sign Language. I've found that many Europeans speak German, so we can often find a connection there. But mostly I just blunder on and probably make a big fool of myself. But what the heck? I do that in English too.

Some fun happens when a kid or parent recognizes me because the person has seen me before as Stone Mountain's Santa. And believe me, it's hard to deny my Santa identity to anyone who's seen me in my Red Suit.

Sometimes it can work in reverse. Once I was in my full Santa gear, eating at a wonderful seafood restaurant in High Point, North Carolina. A lady came up to my table and said, "Hello, Santa. The last time I saw you, you were wearing a blue-and-white-striped outfit."

I was stunned. "My goodness! How in the world did you recognize me?"

"By the twinkle in your eye!" she said.

What a wonderful compliment that was!

Many of the people we see at the theme park are with tour groups, and that adds a new dimension to our encounters. On one occasion there was a large crowd of tour folks waiting for the train, and I (now as Airbrake) asked if there were any rich widows in the group. To my surprise, four women raised their hands. I picked out a pretty lady in the middle and said, "Tell me about it."

She answered, "Well, I own my own home outright, and I have lots of money in the bank. I also have a brand-new Cadillac and a big monthly income."

I said, "Wow! Would you marry me?"

She laughed real loud and said, "Are you kidding me? Marry you and mess all that up? Forget it!" The crowd roared and applauded. I couldn't help but laugh myself.

Every afternoon at 5:30 all of the actors in the Park gather for the Sundown Social event at the gazebo in front of the train station. There is a lot of singing and dancing—and a huge amount of fun. It always ends with the Tennessee Waltz, and the audience is invited to join in. The characters choose partners from the audience while everyone else sways to the music. It's a wonderful time. And it would be even better if I knew how to dance. The kids are often dancing right up front, watching me intently to see what I'm going to do. I did ask a staff member to dance one time, and we did okay, but I could feel the eyes of the audience on my beard and barely kept myself from taking a nosedive.

When the social is over, all the characters are released for the day, except for me. I go back to the train and continue playing with the passengers. Choosing to stay on a bit longer might seem like drudgery to some, but it's not. Occasionally I get to ride the train. I latch on to a kid or friendly adult and accompany the person on the five-mile trip. I have a chance to interact with the child or adult—and he or she has a chance to ask me all the important questions of life, like, "Are you Santa Claus?" "Where are your reindeer?" "Why are you here?" "Am I on the good-kid list?"

I wear a nametag with "Airbrake" on it, and even though I keep pointing to it and asserting, "I'm not Santa," for some reason, folks just don't believe me!

I also have the freedom to walk through Crossroads and see people in other parts of the village. Usually I just walk up to folks and ask how they are doing, where they are from, and how they like our little park. I try to think of myself as the host of the village and to treat people as though they are guests in my home. I always ask if they have any questions about the park or if they need directions or suggestions to get the most out of their visit. I let them know the Park has 3,200 acres, and there are many places scattered throughout that you don't want to miss. It is definitely worth visiting, and it takes at least a couple of days to see it all. So y'all come see us, now, you hear?

## Unanswered Questions

Lots of folks have asked me about the Santa encounters I described in the first volume of *The Red Suit*

*Diaries*. So I'm thinking that you might want to know what has happened to some of the people I wrote about.

One I hear a lot of questions about is the "grown-up little girl," Rachel. Her worst handicap was not her mental disability, but her family's attitude about it. I saw her only once, but I'll never forget the adoring look on her thirtysomething-year-old face as she told me what she wanted for Christmas. Her eyes were full of the kind of wonder you usually see only in very young children.

Her mother told me, "You don't have to mess with her. She ain't right, ain't never been right. You can forget about her." I told her mother that God loved her just like he did all his children, and I would show her God's love with my love. The mother walked away mumbling as her precious daughter sat on my lap and gave me her list. My only regret was that I couldn't just hand her the Barbie doll and other things she asked for, since I didn't think I could trust her family to get them for her.

Though I'm sad that I never saw that childlike woman again, I'm grateful to have had the opportunity to meet and get to know some other wonderful kids. You may remember Cody Cooper. Cody, a near-drowning survivor, was four years old when we met. His mother told me that she didn't know how long Cody would be with them, but that she was going to love him every minute that he lived. And live he did—for sixteen more years. His body finally could not sustain life, and he died peacefully in February 2005.

I had promised his mother years before that I would help with his funeral when the time came and, in spite of my own grief in 2005, I did. It was a glorious celebration of a life that had touched so many people. And it was the dedication of Cody's parents, Judy and Henry, that helped make Cody's life all it could be. They had taken him to Alaska and many places out West. He saw a pod of orcas in the wild—something most kids (and most adults) will never experience. Although Cody never spoke and never had any voluntary movements, he was able to reach others, including me, with a message of love and acceptance of all people.

I also stayed close with Lindsey Brown's family. A year before we met, the Santa at the mall would not touch Lindsey and told her mother to move her out of the way. The next year, not knowing how they had been treated, I called them down off the balcony and took Lindsey out of her wheelchair and into my arms. It didn't matter to me that she had a breathing tube in her nose and a feeding tube in her stomach. Lindsey's mother, Jane, informed me that when her daughter was born, doctors had told her that she would not live for a year. She was four when I met her. Like Cody's mother, Judy, Jane told me she was going to love her child as best she could for as long as she lived. And she would do just that for sixteen whole years.

Lindsey and Cody never met, but I met them within two weeks of one another. And sixteen years later they died within two weeks of one another. I was talking to Jane on the phone at the moment Lindsey died. I was there at the hospice ten minutes later. Like Cody's, her funeral was a celebration of a life filled with love.

## Grieving Together

When little Laura Withers climbed onto my lap at Macy's in 1992, she was the most delightful two-year-old I had ever encountered. In fact, at sixteen she's still delightful. Her dad and mom, Craig and Vicki, are near and dear friends.

On the day my wife, Annie, died, I came home and sent out an email to all our friends. Twenty minutes later, Vicki called and said she was coming over. I told her she was going to do no such thing. It was Christmas Day, and she should spend it with her family. She hung up on me. Fifteen minutes later, the doorbell rang.

I blocked the door with my 270-pound body and told Vicki to go home. She shoved me out of the way and came in the house. Then she grabbed my arms and taught me a valuable lesson. She said, "You are not the only one grieving. I have to grieve too. So let me do something. Anything. Cleaning, dusting, anything."

I told her I had just had the house completely cleaned on Christmas Eve. (That was the only thing Annie had told me she wanted for Christmas.) Then I thought of something. I grabbed a grocery bag out of the pantry and told her she could collect all of Annie's medications and flush them away. I pointed out the places where she could find them, and she went to work. Soon I heard the commode flushing. Then she told me she would take the bottles with her and dispose of them in her trash can at home. She hugged me and left.

The message of her visit—that others were also hurting, sharing my sense of loss—would stay with me for a very long time.

## Revisiting the Early Years

After the first *Red Suit Diaries* was published, I remembered a cute story that I wished I'd included. It happened when I was just starting to think about becoming Santa. I had bought a cheap suit and an even cheaper wig-and-beard set. I thought I looked very authentic. I was wrong. I can't even stand to look at pictures from that time. Fortunately, I've come a long way since then.

Anyway, right after I obtained my first outfit, a friend who was the principal of a small Lutheran school in Decatur, Georgia, asked me to be Santa for a Christmas party. I knew one five-year-old boy who attended that school, but I figured that with my phony beard, wig, and no glasses, there was no way Richard would recognize me.

When I arrived at the school, I went in the appointed door and stepped into a big room. The kids were all gathered on the other side and did not notice that Santa had sneaked in. I took a deep breath and bellowed, "Merry Christmas, everybody!" The reaction: instant screaming and yelling, jumping up and down, and waving of arms.

Above the din I heard a small male voice yell, "Hey, Mr. Butchart!"

I couldn't believe it. How could little Richard make the connection so soon? With my cover blown, I wanted to step out that door again and run away. But I had to be Santa.

The teacher invited me to sit in a big rocking chair and pass out the presents to the kids. I couldn't read the tags without my glasses, so I told her I would need some boys and girls to help me read the tags. Several of them waved their arms and surged forward to help. There, right in the middle, was Richard waving his arm and shouting, "I'll help you, Mr. Butchart! I'll help you, Mr. Butchart!" I decided that I had to take direct action, so I reached for his wrist.

I smiled, pulled him up to me, and whispered playfully in his ear, "Richard, if you call me Mr. Butchart one more time, I'll break your arm!"

He pulled his head back, his eyes wide. "Okay, Santa Claus!" he said.

I know what you're thinking, and you're right. That was a mean thing to say, and if I had to do it over, I would say it differently. I was a rookie then. I had a lot to learn. I *still* have a lot to learn, and I hope I never quit learning how to do Santa—and how to do life.

## Continuing Education

One lesson I am still learning is to be ready for the unexpected. You can just never anticipate what a child might say or do. This one little guy looked about as average as they come. He was just standing, staring, and taking me in when I gestured for him to come to me. He stepped up on my stool and swung his way onto my right leg. As soon as he sat down, he exclaimed, "Whoa! You're a lot bigger than I expected."

I leaned back a little and responded, "Well, how big were you expecting?"

He raised his hands and held them about a foot apart. "About this big," he said, his eyes like saucers.

That one took me a moment. "Oh," I said, "that's how big I am on television. In real life I'm much bigger."

He paused for a minute, then finally said, "Okay. Well, here's my list." And he launched into a long, highly sophisticated list of wishes, in order of preference.

## The First Claus

There have been some constants in all of my Santa Claus encounters. I still hear the same questions again and again, and I still answer them as though it's the first time I've ever heard them. Many times this gives me a chance to give a minisermon about the significance of Christmas, and I welcome the opportunity. One of my favorite questions has to do with the roots of Santa's role in the Christmas celebration.

A lot of people don't know the legend of Santa Claus, so they have the mistaken opinion that Santa is a pagan figure with no relationship to the birth of Jesus Christ. Many of them have strong feelings against having Santa included in church celebrations. Unfortunately, some Santas don't know the history either and do a poor job of explaining the connection.

More Pages from the Red Suit Diaries

The details are a bit obscure, since they go back hundreds of years. But there is no disputing the fact that the legend of Santa is based on a real man—and not just any man, but a bishop of the early church. His parents had died in one of the devastating plagues that swept Europe. This man, whose name was Nicholas, was left with a large inheritance. And though he was just a boy when his parents passed away, he found himself with the responsibility of caring for the church in his hometown of Myra, a small village in what is modern-day Turkey. Nicholas grew into a strong, healthy man and was very active in his community. When he was elected bishop, he was still quite young.

Aware of many needy families in his small village, he used his money to make their lives easier. Sometimes a family needed a specific item, and it would miraculously appear overnight. For example, there was a poor family with four daughters and no way to pay a dowry so that the daughters could marry. As the girls matured one by one, the money required to pay the dowry would mysteriously appear. The coins would be found in the elder sister's shoes or stockings, which were hung by the fireplace to dry.

Acts of generosity spread throughout the parish—and so did theories about where the funds and items had come from. Nicholas always crept through the village very late at night, and since he knew everyone, even all the dogs, he was not confronted by a single creature. After the "miracles" had been told and retold, the stories began to spread beyond the borders of his country. Finally he was unmasked, but the legends, now attributed to Bishop Nicholas, continued to spread.

His parishioners began to call him Saint Nicholas. Years later the church would canonize him, making the title official. As the stories and legends spread throughout Europe, his name was transliterated. From *Sint Nikolaas* (Dutch for Saint Nicholas), it became the nickname *Sinter Klaas* in the Netherlands and was ultimately brought to the New World by Dutch immigrants. Eventually the name was anglicized to Santa Claus. This is, of course, a very abridged history. The full story of this man is quite remarkable. Perhaps that's the reason there are more churches in the world named for Saint Nicholas than for any other saint.

Clement Clark Moore (or Henry Livingston Jr., as some contend) wrote the poem "Account of a Visit from St. Nicholas" (later known as "The Night before Christmas"). This poem and the illustrations by Thomas Nast, a Civil War–era cartoonist, helped refine the modern image of Santa Claus. Then Haddon Sunbloom, the artist for the Coca-Cola advertisements of the 1930s and '40s, further developed the image into the Santa Claus we recognize today. The legend of Santa Claus has nothing to do with paganism and nothing to do with the Antichrist, but many people think this because they don't know the real history of Santa Claus. That's the reason I enjoy being Santa and sharing his true message of love, acceptance, and generosity.

## The Marshmallow Boy

Even though it's my job as Santa to gives gifts, numerous gifts have come *my* way over the years. One specific story comes to mind. About twelve years ago, my elf Pete and I were holding forth on the throne at Stone Mountain Park when a young boy showed up carrying a white bag with two toasted marshmallows in it. He said, "These are for y'all," handed me the bag, and walked away. Pete and I looked around to see if there were parents involved but didn't spot any likely suspects. We figured the boy had roasted the marshmallows at the bonfire behind the train station and had brought them to share with us. Not to look ungrateful, we gobbled them up while they were still warm.

A week later he came by again. More marshmallows—and another quick exit. Still no sign of any parents. Another week, and more marshmallows! Pete dubbed our visitor "The Marshmallow Boy," and that would be our name for him for the eight years that he kept his routine. No matter where the Park set us up each year, we could count on The Marshmallow Boy to keep bringing us his special treats.

It took me several years before I finally spotted a lady who looked as though she could be his mom. We were walking outside. The boy had just handed me the bag, and there she was in the background. I asked her if she was his mom. She said yes. I hugged her and asked their names. She said his name was Lee Hagan and her name was Ann. I told her about our name for him, and she got a huge kick out of that. She told me that they lived just outside the west gate to Stone Mountain and considered the Park to be their front yard. She had always kept Lee in sight when he was bringing us his marshmallow gifts, even though we'd never noticed her.

From then on, I saw both of them when he stopped by. Then, during the summer I became Airbrake, Ann introduced me to her husband, Jim. He was a delightful guy. He had just retired as a DeKalb County EMT and was going to be a park ranger. I saw him on duty from time to time.

Lee was growing up fast. His parents were both slim but not tall, and he soon surpassed them. When he was sixteen, he got his driver's license and began to restore an old car. He came by and kept me posted on his progress. Then his interest switched to motorcycles.

The next thing I knew, he showed up at the train in the uniform of a park ranger. What a fine young man he was becoming!

Then came the nicest surprise of all. Pete and I got invitations to attend the Court of Honor when Lee received his Eagle Scout award. We attended together, and it was an evening of great pride as I heard all the ways our Marshmallow Boy had grown into a terrific young man and wonderful citizen. I knew his parents were enormously proud—because I felt a measure of vicarious pride myself.

## Second-Generation Encounters

The season of 2004 was particularly difficult for me because Annie was in the hospital for most of it, and my mind and heart were not completely focused on other people's kids. But I was determined that every child would have a jolly-old-Saint-Nick moment, no matter what.

One evening I had just come back from a break and hadn't yet sat down when a woman approached me and said, "I've been bringing my daughter to see you for fourteen years. She was six when we came the first time." She gestured to a lovely young lady. I shook her hand, and then she hugged me.

Her mom said, "She has a surprise for you." The young lady hustled off the set and around the corner. I decided to keep standing and see what would happen.

In a moment she came back—carrying a baby! She walked up, handed me the newborn girl, and said, "I wanted my baby to come see my Santa for her first Santa pictures."

She did not know I was already an emotional wreck, but she found out when I completely lost it, posing for a standing picture with Mom and Grandma, then carrying the little one to the throne and letting them take a whole bunch of pictures. This was my first second-generation visit. I was bawling like a baby, and the one I was holding was looking quizzically at me. I could just hear her thinking, *What's the matter, Big Boy?* I'm sure her family was asking the same question. I handed the baby back to Mom and thanked her. I was truly grateful she had come.

That was my only second-generationer until a year later, when virtually the same scene played out again. This grandma also told me she had first brought her daughter to see Santa when she was six and that their family had repeated the event every year for fifteen years. She said she had an eight-by-ten print of every year's picture. They were framed and on the wall of their main hallway all year round. She was very excited about having a new picture with the mother and the grandbaby together.

After that shot, Grandma gathered their other two kids and Grandpa, and we did a family portrait. Mom was kind enough to say that I looked exactly the same in every one of their annual pictures. (I told her that I was already old when she started saving them.) This time I did maintain control during the sweet moment. It just isn't proper for Santa to cry like a baby!

# sharing joy

## Educating Santa

One of my long-standing personal rules has been that I should never be seen in public with another Santa. I have walked out of many stores and restaurants when I've spotted another Santa there, because I don't want to cause any trauma for the kids who might see us.

But at the same time, I'd heard about a place in Midland, Michigan, that holds a Santa training school each year. At first, the idea of being with a group of Santas just didn't fit into my preconceived ideas of playing the role. I found myself wanting to learn what was being taught there, but not wanting to be seen with a crowd of white-bearded wonders.

My first book, TV appearances, and local and national newspaper articles had brought me letters and emails from Santas all over the country. In the summer of 2003 I received a call from Gary Casey, a local guy. He told me that a nationally known Santa from California was coming to Atlanta in September to conduct a one-day seminar for Santas. When I heard this, I decided I would bite the bullet and go.

It was a tremendous experience. Even after fourteen years of being Santa, I still learned a lot and met a bunch of terrific guys. The speaker was Tim Connaghan, a delightful man filled with energy, love for the Lord, and an earnestness that was infectious to all seventy Santas and Mrs. Clauses in attendance. Because he'd read my book, Tim invited me to do a twenty-minute presentation on the real meaning of Christmas. It was an opportunity for me to talk about the Lord to all those Santas and encourage them to use every chance they got to tell kids and adults about the roots of Santa's history and the true meaning of Christmas.

Tim had an audacious name for his seminar: International University of Santa Claus, and he conferred the degree of Bachelor of Clausology on each graduate. I enjoyed it so much that I decided to go back the next year and to apply to the Michigan Santa School when I had the chance. I did Tim's seminar again, with Annie, in September 2004. She was not really well enough to go but she didn't want to disappoint me. We had a good time together, and she learned a lot about how to improve her portrayal of Mrs. Claus. She was really tickled when she got her Bachelor of Mrs. Clausology degree. She called the whole day a "real hoot."

Soon after that, Annie's health went sour, and I spent my time taking care of her. I forgot all about the Santa School in Michigan. The summer of 2005, after Annie had died, I was beginning to come back to life again when a Santa friend in High Point, North Carolina, called to remind me about the Michigan school. I applied immediately and started planning the trip.

October in Michigan, I was to learn, can be spectacularly beautiful and unexpectedly cool. It was a little of both for the three days at the Charles W. Howard Santa School. But the cooler northern weather was made completely bearable by the warmth of the crowd of a hundred students and the wonderful hospitality of the school dean, Tom Valent, and his wife, Holly, who served as registrar. They had assembled a formidable array of speakers and entertainers. In no time at all, they had inspired a warm camaraderie among all these look-alikes. We stood and sang songs to greet each speaker, then sang again to thank them when they finished. There could not have been a happier, more enthusiastic crowd. I learned a lot—maybe not so much about how to be Santa, but a lot about what a wonderful group of men and women were playing the role. There wasn't a grouch or a grinch anywhere to be found.

Charles W. Howard was the original Macy's store and parade Santa. He set such a high standard of performance excellence that other Santas sought him out for training and advice. He decided to start a school to teach men who aspired to the role. His first class was in 1947. In 1997 he passed the mantle of leadership to Tom and Holly Valent, and they moved the school to a wonderful downtown site in the charming little town of Midland, Michigan. Their Santa House is open for tours year-round, and it's where the town's annual Christmas program is held. Every kid for miles around knows that Santa comes to the Santa House to take orders for Christmas gifts each year.

We Santas were all over the little town of Midland. I discovered that nearly all the residents knew about the school and looked forward to the week when "class" was in session and the town was full of Santas. We went on field trips to several places, noteworthy among them the town of Frankenmuth, Michigan, with its famous Bronner's Christmas Wonderland, the "World's Largest Christmas Store."

We virtually took over the large dining room in a Bavarian-style restaurant in town. The other diners, kids included, seemed enchanted by the sight of so many Santas in one place. While we waited for our food, we broke into song and sang several of our favorites, completely captivating our involuntary audience. After the meal we wandered in small groups around the town and had so much fun in the shops and on the street that all my anxiety of being with a group of Santas melted away. Finally I relaxed, went with the flow, and found myself having an absolutely wonderful time.

I was strolling down the sidewalk with three other Santas when a little guy came up to me, pointed, and said, "I think you are the real one."

I couldn't resist and responded, "Why do you think so?"

He said, "You just look more real than the rest of them."

He had no idea what a huge compliment he had just given me. I leaned over, put my index finger to my lips and, looking furtively up and down the sidewalk, said, "Shhh! Don't tell anybody, okay? It has to be a secret."

He said, "Okay!" and hustled back to his parents waiting farther down the sidewalk. I heard him shout to them as he ran, "I told you it was him, Mom." It had worked again. I never answered him directly, yet sent him on his way convinced of his answer. His faith and trust were restored, if they had ever even wavered. I could see that being with a group of Santas did not necessarily detract from the opportunity to share God's love. It may have even enhanced it.

The trip to Bronner's was completely awe-inspiring. There were more than four acres of merchandise—all Christmas and mostly religious. I was in Santa heaven! With that many Santas in the store, it was not a surprise that there was a festive air. Everyone was having a wonderful time, probably me most of all. We were there for only an hour and a half—just enough time for me to grab a massive pile of Christmas stuff off the shelves and arrange for it to be shipped home. I had to swallow hard when I handed my credit card to the clerk after she announced, "That will be $352.80." Ouch! But there was no way I could put any of it back.

One of the Santas gave a business card to one of the kids, and in a flash there were crowds of kids dashing all through the store, asking the Santas for cards and collecting them by the handful. Unfortunately, I had only a few cards with me.

One girl rushed up and said, "Gimme one of your cards!"

I told her I didn't have any more.

"Why not?" she demanded.

When I told her I had given them all away, she said angrily, "Well, next time bring more!" Good advice.

Two other cardless Santas and I decided to sit down in a traffic-free spot. We were talking when a little girl named Christina came up to us holding a card. She started comparing our faces with the one on the card. One of the guys asked what she was doing, and she said, "I am searching for the real Santa. This is his picture."

When she turned the picture around, it was me! She was holding my card! She placed the card in front of us and compared the picture and the faces. When she held the card up to me, she screamed. "That's him! I found him! This is the real Santa!"

If you love Christmas and are ever in Michigan, don't miss Bronner's. If you are not in Michigan, go there. It's worth the trip.

## Santa Convention

The event in Michigan doesn't constitute the biggest crowd of Santas I would ever be a part of. Years ago seminar speaker Tim Connaghan assembled a few Santas for a social event in California. He chartered the group with the highfalutin' title of Amalgamated Order of Real Bearded Santas (AORBS). Later he opened the group to national membership, then decided to conduct an international convention in Branson, Missouri, in the summer of 2006.

It was a massive undertaking, which he began by recruiting volunteers to serve in various capacities on the convention committee. Cliff Snider, my Santa friend in High Point, asked me to help him on the committee managing vendor participation. That was a piece of cake for me, as I had a lot of experience with trade shows. Cliff and I struck a deal. He would keep up with the vendors and their requirements. I would deal with the hotel, prepare the rooms for the vendors, help them get set up on the day before the convention, and support them during the four days.

On July 4 I drove out to Branson. I had recruited Dewaine Fisher, a rookie Santa from far north Georgia, as my copilot. The drive out there was easier than either of us had thought. There was minimal traffic on the interstate. In a couple of restaurants and gas stations we had some fun encounters as people wondered about this old Santa and his obviously younger sidekick. We told them he was my protégé.

The vendor setup went really well, and that spirit of Santa camaraderie appeared right away. I kept checking with the registration desk for attendance numbers, which topped out at almost four hundred Santas—the largest gathering of real-bearded Santas ever assembled in one place. One fun part for me was that a very large number of them were bald, wore glasses, and generally looked a lot like me. One of them was a dead ringer. When I first looked at him, I thought I was looking into a mirror. Is that scary or what? I'll tell you how scary it was. I was standing in the lobby, and a nice-looking lady came up to me, grabbed my arm, and said, "Come on, we're going to miss the bus." When I hesitated a moment, she turned, studied me for a moment, then said, "Oh no, you're not my husband!"

I answered quickly, "Yeah, I know, but which bus are we going on?"

Very early on Friday morning, the entire crowd of Santas and Mrs. Clauses gathered for a parade in a shopping area a block from the hotel. More than four hundred people showed up in red uniforms. The parade was timed for the network morning news shows, and some of the crews were there. We gathered behind the shopping area and, on signal, walked to the front and packed into a small courtyard. Several photographers and videographers were posted on a lift device high above us, and we stood around while they filmed and taped us. The results were quite a sight to behold. I wound up in the very back of the crowd and did not make it into any of the pictures that were printed and offered for sale. But it was a huge kick, and if there were any vestiges of my phobia about being in the company of other Santas, they were sure gone now!

Two people showed up in something other than Santa red that day, and one of them was my friend Cliff. He wore an authentic replica of the stars-and-stripes suit that first appeared in the Thomas Nast cartoons in the early 1800s. The other was a Santa from Pennsylvania, a history buff who wore a replica of an early European version of a *Sinter Klaas* outfit. I found out that you actually *can* stand out in a crowd of Santa Clauses.

We had lots of classes on various subjects of interest to Santas—costuming, hair care, and dealing with difficult children and parents. We were able to attend five of the famous Branson entertainer shows, and every one of them was a spectacular experience. Santas were everywhere. We had such a good time.

A group of us were eating in a restaurant when a mother came by and thanked us for being there. She said her two boys had stopped fussing when we came in—and had been good the whole time. They had decided that they needed to be on their best behavior for so many Santas.

One grown man in his early fifties stopped at our table, looked at me, and declared, "I am still disappointed that I did not get the car I asked for last Christmas."

I stood up and said, "Oh no, did I forget that? I'm sorry. Here, you can have it now." I pulled a toy car out of my pocket and handed it to him.

He was stunned and stood for a moment looking at the Matchbox-sized vehicle. Then he said, "I wanted one I could ride in."

"Well," I retorted, "I am a toy maker, not an automobile manufacturer. I don't make cars you can ride in."

"Oh," he answered, handing the toy back to me. "Give this to a kid who will enjoy it." He broke into a huge smile as he stuck out his hand. "Thank you so much; this was a fun moment. Thank you."

I shook his hand, and he went on his way. Adults can have fun encounters with Santa too!

Several people armed with cameras followed us around as they "covered the event." One of them was a tiny lady with a video camera, and I began to realize that she was taking a lot of footage of me. Finally I confronted her. She said she was from Voice of America and she had asked Tim for an example of a Santa who best exemplified what Santa was all about. He told her about me and my ministry and history and referred her to my websites. She was doing a minidocumentary about me and promised she would let me see what she did with the footage.

The convention closed on Sunday at noon, and Tim had decided we needed to have a "church service" to close it out. When he asked me if I would lead the service, I quickly agreed. I never pass up an opportunity to make an appeal for Santas to remember that they are representing a man of God, Bishop Nicholas of

Myra, and are ultimately representing our Lord and Savior, Jesus Christ.

I reminded them that Jesus had been asked what the greatest commandment is and that he had answered, "Love the Lord your God with all your heart and with all your soul and with all your mind." He had continued by saying, "And the second [commandment] is like it: 'Love your neighbor as yourself.'" That is our role as Santas: to demonstrate the love that Christ showed us and to pass it on to every child and adult we meet. I told my audience that if they had a problem with that, they should shave their beards and turn in their Red Suits, because that is what being Santa is all about. It is all about love.

## A Lost Sleigh

After the Branson convention, I stayed in town for two extra days to sign books in a charming Christmas shop there. I also visited Silver Dollar City, a sister park to my own Stone Mountain Park back home.

We didn't have a lot of time but we used it well. Dewaine, my younger fellow Santa, rode the roller coasters over and over while I wandered around the shops and outdoor shows. I did ride the train—to see if it differed from the one back home.

Late in the afternoon, we saw a huge black cloud approaching and hustled for the exit. We made it there before the rain, but there were only three shuttles to take all the visitors to their cars. Suddenly the downpour was upon us. We huddled under my golf umbrella and waited through several cycles of trams.

Finally we scrambled aboard. But we got very wet in the open-sided tram. Then, to my horror, I could not remember where I had parked the car. I knew which lot it was in, but I saw nothing that looked familiar. I let Dewaine use the umbrella while I struck out in the most driving rain I had ever experienced. In moments I was soaked to the drawers and wetter than I ever was during the monsoon seasons in Vietnam. For twenty minutes I wandered around and never found my car. Several people tried to be helpful as they drove by. Others lowered their windows a sliver and shouted things like "What happened, Santa, lose your sleigh?" Or "Did your reindeer take off without you?" I did not respond with what I wanted to say, believe me. After all, what had I just said about showing Christian love to all?

Finally I went back to the shelter where Dewaine was waiting, and he began to look. Earlier I had dropped him at the entrance and parked the car myself, but he found it in just a few minutes—barely fifty yards away from the shelter, though in the opposite direction.

There was a lesson here for Santa: always remember where you park your sleigh! It was also a reminder that I really am not Santa Claus, just an ordinary man with ordinary foibles.

A couple of weeks after the convention, I got an email from Tim with a link to Voice of America. I clicked on the site and was able to see what the lady shooting the video had produced. She had done a beautiful job of editing the footage, and the narration described a person I would really like to be. I was floored. But I was even more stunned when I found that it was being broadcast in more than forty countries around the world—and had been translated into nearly twenty languages! I could not help but think that here was this country boy from down a dirt road in North Carolina, and his story was being told all around the world. My mama would have been so proud. It was a very humbling experience. It also reminded me of a favorite line from Yakov Smirnoff, whose stand-up show we'd just seen in Branson: "What a country!"

I would attend Santa Tim's seminar again. I think the biggest lesson I have learned is that the Santa population in general is made up of kind, loving, caring men and women who show the love of the Lord to every kid they meet, on or off the throne.

## Festivals and Craft Shows

Any time I am out in public, I must be prepared either to be Santa or to reject the role. Although I am well aware of this, I am often reminded that I am onstage and must be ready to perform when needed.

I went with some friends to the Milford Memories celebration in downtown Milford, Michigan. The town closes off several blocks, and craftspeople and artists set up tents to sell their wares. There are also food booths, entertainers, and large crowds. As we made our way among the tents, several of the vendors called me Santa and made other comments. Several people posed the most popular question: "Has anybody ever told you that you look like Santa Claus?" Here I am, in a full white beard and a red shirt with "Santa" embroidered above the pocket. I restrained myself from answering, "Well, duh!" I just chose to play dumb and say, "Really? You really think so? How about that!"

Some asked, "What are you doing here, Santa?" Answer: "I've got to vacation somewhere!" Another answer: "I'm checking my list. This is a great place to see if kids are being good boys and girls."

Others asked, "Who is making the toys, Santa?"

Answer: "The elves have everything under control. I trained them well, so I don't have to be there all the time."

Many people just waved and said, "Hi, Santa." I waved back and said "Hello" or "Hi, there" or something equally as creative.

At one point I felt a tug on the back of my shirt. I turned around and saw three young boys looking expectantly at me. The biggest one stepped closer and said, "Are you Santa Claus?"

I leaned over to them and said, "No, I'm the Easter Bunny."

"No, you're not!" came the three-part-harmony reply.

"Oh, why not?" I asked.

"You just don't look like the Easter Bunny," the oldest retorted.

"Really? Who do I look like?" I leaned forward again.

"You look like Santa Claus," the oldest answered.

I leaned even closer to them, bringing my finger to

my lips, and said, "Shhh, don't tell anybody. Okay? I'm on vacation."

They all nodded vigorously and disappeared into the crowd.

A few moments later, I felt another tug. The smallest of the three was standing there. I leaned forward as he cupped his hand to his mouth, looked around, and asked confidentially, "Can I just tell my dad?"

"Okay, sure. You can tell your dad," I answered. He whirled around and was gone.

I never go to one of these events without trying some of the food. At Milford it was the roasted corn on the cob that caught my eye, and I absolutely loved the taste of it. I knew there would be little chance of having that again, so I did what any red-blooded Santa would do. I ate another one.

There was a troop of Civil War reenactors camped out in a meadow near the craft tents, and we walked over to see their encampment. They were well established, with well-equipped and authentic tents, cooking gear, and accessories. The wives, children, and camp followers were there too. While the men practiced drilling and tactical maneuvering, the women were cooking the next meal. We spent some time talking with the women about life in the camp, and they stayed in character as they described their activities.

None of them said a word about Santa or Christmas for a while, but then one of them noted, "We have Santa in our lives too." I remembered from my history studies that Santa became an important figure just before the Civil War, when the poem "A Visit from St. Nicholas" was being published and becoming a favorite. The woman went on to tell me that they have an encampment at Christmastime, and one of their members dresses in an authentic period Santa outfit and plays the role for all the kids and families. It reminded me that Santa has been around a long time and that even in those worst of days and conditions, he provided a measure of happiness for those fighting that miserable war.

We continued to wander around the fair for a while and then left to get some real food. We settled into a booth and immediately caught the attention of two siblings sitting nearby. They stared. I waved. They waved back and seemed completely absorbed by what they saw. In a few minutes, their dad went to the men's room. I gave him a moment, then went myself. I asked him his kids' names, and he told me: Katie and Brian. I went back into the dining room.

As I passed their booth, I stopped and asked the young lad, "Have you been good to your sister, Brian?"

The sister jumped and exclaimed, "He knows your name, Brian!"

I turned to her and said, "Of course I know his name, Katie. I know a lot of things. Like I know you have been picking on Brian some too."

Her mouth flew open and her eyes grew wide.

"That is why you have to always be a good girl, Katie, and a good boy, Brian. You just never know who is watching you. Can you remember that?"

They both nodded sheepishly.

"Good. Keep it up." And I went to my seat.

The family left before we did, and as they went by

our booth, they each told me good-bye. It occurred to me that they will have quite a story to tell their grandchildren!

## Grandpa Santa

Speaking of grandchildren, folks ask me from time to time what my own grandchildren think about having Santa as a grandpa. I do have grandchildren—five of them. They range in age from six to twenty-one. Joshua, the twenty-one-year-old, and his nineteen-year-old sister, Jessica, carry my picture card with them and love to tell their friends about me. They report that most of their friends simply don't believe that the guy in the picture is their Gramps. They have a different last name, so the words on the back of my card don't mean much to their friends.

Thirteen-year-old Kristen and eleven-year-old Taylor have a lot of fun trying to convince their friends that their grandpa is Santa, a fact they believe with all their hearts. Sometimes I show up at the sports events where they are cheerleaders and add some credibility to their claims. They seem to love it.

Then there is Logan, only six and still trying to decide what she believes. Sometimes one of the grand-kids will ask me the dreaded question, "Are you *really* Santa Claus, Grandpa?" I answer the same way I answer other kids. I say, "Don't you tell anybody, okay? It has to be a secret."

I am also the father of three boys and one girl. Paul, the oldest, is now a dead ringer for his old man. In a year or so he will be a great Santa in his own right. When he was a little guy, his favorite thing was to ride through the neighborhood where we were living in Kailua, Hawaii, and see all the Christmas lights. He would stand on the backseat of the car, peering out the window, pointing, and saying, "Yook at the yights, Dad. Yook at the yights, Mom!" He would get so excited.

When Mark, my second son, was about three, he became an amateur mechanic and professional snoop. He could not stand seeing a closed door, drawer, or box. He *had* to open it to see what was inside. He would never mess with what he found, however. Once he had seen it, he would quietly close the lid or door and leave it alone. When we visited friends or family, he always drove our hosts crazy by snooping through things. My older brother's wife would follow him around, trying to herd him back to where everyone else was. But soon he would return to where he had left off and continue snooping.

He also loved to take things apart and see how they worked. He disassembled just about everything he could get his hands on. One year as Christmas approached, I told him that if he kept breaking things, Santa was going to bring him a brick, a concrete block, and a two-by-four. I told him that a few times, and then a couple of weeks later, I took him to see Santa at the mall. When it was his turn, he jumped up on Santa's lap and, when he was asked the expected question, responded, "I want a brick, a concrete block, and a two-by-four." The look on Santa's face was classic.

On Christmas morning, I made sure Mark got what he had asked for. I wrapped up a brick, a concrete block, and a two-foot length of two-by-four. When he came down from his bedroom, he ran to the tree, picked up the brick, and started to unwrap it. He dropped it before it was unwrapped, and the brick broke in two. When he tried to pick up the concrete block, he dropped it, breaking it as well. He was able to unwrap the two-by-four without breaking it. Of course there were also toys, stuffed animals, and a couple of games. But he was sad that what he had really wanted was broken. (But so were the rest of his gifts within a couple of weeks.)

## Here Comes Santa Claus

"The Grand Entrance of Santa Claus" has become a nightly feature at Stone Mountain Park. We call it the Parade, since all the characters performing in the various shows precede the sleigh for the walk through our replica village of Crossroads.

The sleigh is made of plywood attached to one of the Kawasaki work carts used by the maintenance crew—a valiant attempt at a replica sleigh. It is painted red and white and trimmed with golden filigree. The sleigh is outlined and covered with lights. Out in front of the sleigh is a pair of metal beams that support five of those white lawn reindeer that are filled with lights and whose heads move either from side to side or up and down. The lights on this incredible operation are illuminated via a gas-powered generator mounted underneath the sleigh's wooden frame. It is loud and smells of burning motor oil. One of our characters, dressed in an elf outfit, drives, while Santa stands, supported by the high sides of the sleigh.

The parade starts at the Great Barn and travels down the main street of Crossroads, which, even on days with the worst of weather, is lined with a crowd of adoring spectators awaiting a glimpse of the "jolly old elf." We get a big kick out of waving and shout-ing, "Merry Christmas!" to folks along the route. The view of the millions of lights in the village is quite spectacular from up in the sleigh. I absolutely love that sight, so it's easy to be jolly.

Most nights there's at least one Santa heckler in the crowd. Comments like "Happy Holidays, not Merry Christmas, Santa!" are not uncommon. If I answer at all, I usually say, "In Crossroads, it is Merry Christmas!" Occasionally some smart aleck will comment about the reindeer: "Your reindeer are getting skinny, Santa. You need to feed them better." My best response is, "They are being fed 110 volts AC at 60 amps. That's all they need."

But that is not always true. Sometimes the cantankerous generator shuts down, cutting power to the lights on the sleigh and reindeer. If it won't start after a few tries, we just make the trip in the dark. That brings on another round of heckling, but it is all in fun, and we enjoy that too. It breaks up the routine for sure.

Everybody knows there are "eight tiny reindeer," plus Rudolph. I just told you that we have only five. The one in front has a red bulb on his nose, so everyone knows who he is. We get a lot of comments about missing reindeer. I can't tell folks that initially we tried longer beams with nine reindeer, but the weight of so many reindeer in the front caused the rear wheels of the sleigh to lift off the ground. And even when we ballasted it to keep the wheels down, the length made it very tricky to steer down the narrow streets of town. We compromised with five reindeer. Sometimes reality takes priority over fantasy.

## Visiting Friends

One of my favorite appearances is my annual trip to a gift shop in High Point, North Carolina. Just by seeing the kids and parents there for a few minutes once a year, I have made some great friends. On my most recent visit I was invited to have dinner at the home of a dentist, Joel Gentry, and his wife, Shirene. This was the sixth time they had extended that courtesy. Shirene asked me in advance what I would like to eat, and I told her very truthfully that I had learned that anything she put on her table was delicious. As long as there was no liver, sugar, or trans fats, I would love it.

The Gentrys showed me a photo album that documents the "Santa visits" of their sons, Austin and Forrest, from the time they were infants. The first time I saw Austin, he was a newborn. Now he is a strapping, handsome fourteen-year-old. That evening Austin was going to a school dance and was very excited. As I studied the album, I could see that I really don't look as though I have aged. I told Shirene it must be because of my genes!

I also enjoy visiting the family of Bob and Sandra Wilkinson. For the past several years, they have taken me to a seafood restaurant for dinner. I can count on a lot of laughter around the table as we catch up on events in our lives during the preceding year. This last time, though, we discussed a somber subject as they told me about Sandra's battle with cancer. She is doing well and is very optimistic, praising the Lord for his hand in her treatment.

We always have a great time interacting with the other patrons at the restaurant. It isn't every day that you see an authentic-looking Santa in his full regalia, sitting at the next table as you dine. At least in that outfit no one tells me, "Hey, you like Santa Claus!" This time several people brought their kids by to see me, and some even filmed the moment. One mother said, "Thanks, Santa, you just saved us a trip to the mall to get that picture."

The food was wonderful, and the fellowship and encounters were even more wonderful. The Wilkinson grandchildren, Drew and Riley, have grown up having supper with Santa one night a year. Those kids are delightful and beautiful. Riley is five this year, and his dimpled cheeks are becoming more prominent. He told me that a girl in his class told the teacher that he has holes in his cheeks and is so cute! He really is cute, and she will not be the last girl who will think so.

Usually I don't include stories in my diaries that don't happen to me personally, but this one is just too precious to pass up. In the course of the evening, Bob told me about a four-year-old boy who was taken to see another Santa. When the Santa asked him what he wanted for Christmas, the boy hesitated a few moments before blurting out, "A bug zapper!" Santa looked at his parents, but they had no explanation for this request.

## Kylie

The first time I saw her, she was struggling to walk to me. She was dragging one foot, and one arm was drawn up tight to her side. It was 2002. Kylie was five, but she was small for her age. I helped her up onto my lap. She snuggled tight against me and laid her head on my shoulder. She sighed heavily, and I was sure it was because she was worn out from the exertion of walking. I said hello and asked how she was doing. She answered, "Better now."

I asked her what was going on. She answered slowly, "I have a brain tumor, Santa. I've already had two surgeries, and I have more to go; then I'll be well."

My heart nearly stopped. How could this beautiful child be dealing with such a terrible subject so simply and confidently? I hugged her closer and responded. "Tell me your name, sweetie."

"My name is Kylie, Santa."

"I am going to be praying for you, Kylie. In fact, let's pray right now." I bowed my head, and she put her forehead against my cheek. I prayed a prayer of contrition and petition of healing for this lovely child. I didn't want to stop praying, but knew I could not keep it up forever. I was speaking quietly so only Kylie and I could hear my voice, but I knew that the words were reaching the ears of the One who needed to hear them.

While I was praying, Kylie's grandmother took a picture of us. I did not know it had happened, and when I opened my eyes, Kylie's grandmother was not there. Kylie told me her list and as she did, her grandmother came back into the store. Her little brother Connor, who obviously adores his sister, and their cousin Brittany, who adores both of them, had been patiently waiting.

There were some other kids in line too. So finally I had to let Kylie go on her way. I kept my promise and prayed for her often over the next year.

Annie went with me for the visit to High Point in 2004. It was a new venue for me—in a children's clothing store called Tadpoles. I was afraid Kylie's family would not hear about the new place and might not make it.

At one point I was concentrating on a boy sitting on my left leg and was aware that Annie was interacting with someone on the bench to my right. I let the little fellow down and he toddled off. Then Annie said, "Here is Kylie, Santa."

I turned and my eyes watered. She looked terrific. Her color was better, and she had grown a lot and gained some weight. I hugged her and Annie too, so tightly I nearly melted them together. I looked at her grandmother, a delightfully loving woman named Angie Bean. She was grinning broadly and nodding her head vigorously. "Does this mean what I think it means, Gran?" I asked.

She said, "Yes it does, Santa. Kylie is doing much, much better! The tumor is benign and most of it is gone now. She is relearning a few things, but she is much better." She also handed me an eight-by-ten print of the photo she had taken two years earlier of Kylie and me praying together. It is the most treasured of all the photos in my album.

More tears rolled down my face and I shouted, "Praise the Lord!" for all to hear and hugged everybody again, Gran included. I promised to keep praying for Kylie and told her granny to keep me posted by email.

The year 2005 was an agonizing one. It hurt to go to High Point without Annie, but a promise is a promise. This time when Kylie came in the door, I saw that huge smile immediately. I got out of my chair and walked to her to give her a hug. Then we walked together back to the chair.

She gave me a full report, and her gran confirmed it. Kylie was still improving and her speech was much better. She told me she was being monitored periodically, and everything was going well. She was walking a lot better, although she still had a bit of a limp. She told me she was sorry about Annie. I told her that now we both had an angel in heaven looking out for us. She liked that idea.

Another year passed, and at ten Kylie is becoming a lovely young lady. I am not sure how many more years I will be able to go to High Point, but Kylie will always be in my prayers. I am sure I will get reports from Granny Angie from time to time. I have always known that prayer works. But to see a walking testimony to its power is an awesome thing. And to have been a part of it is a humbling experience. Thank you, Lord, for using me to bring joy and happiness to this wonderful little girl and her family.

## A New Venue

I am new to the Hill Skills Crafts and Art Exhibition in Greenville, South Carolina. It is hosted by Rachel McKaughan, who was raised just a mile away from us when we lived in Guilford County, North Carolina. We had not seen each other in more than fifty years. My brother Peter had been in touch with her, and he told her I was a published author. She told him she needed an author for this year's show, and when I found out, I decided to go for at least part of the four-day session. I did the appearance in my Santa suit and had a tremendous time signing books and having my picture taken with visitors.

I was not swamped with customers, so I spent some time touring the booths and passing out brochures for my book. People were quite surprised to see Santa walking aimlessly around the place, while I was shocked by the quality of the offerings of the crafters. I tried my best to resist buying some things but finally did succumb to temptation and bought a couple of Santa artifacts to add to my collection.

In the booth next to mine there was a nice lady selling potted orchids. I have always been fascinated by those beautiful flowers and was able to work a trade with her for one of my books. She started to read the book right

More Pages from the Red Suit Diaries

away. As the day wore on, I could hear her chuckling, laughing, and even crying out loud. It looked like she hated to stop reading to wait on customers. I considered it to be a big endorsement for my writing.

When I got the orchid home, I did my best to follow the woman's instructions. But like most plants I have ever had, I managed to kill it off in just a few months.

&

Another great craft show is the annual Yellow Daisy Arts and Crafts Festival. It takes place the weekend after Labor Day and has been a Stone Mountain Park tradition for at least twenty-five years. There are more than four hundred crafters there and a careful gleaning process selects the very best of the nearly one thousand artisans who apply, so the quality of the products is a wonder to behold. The booths are spread along paved pathways in the woods and the stroll among the booths is an absolute delight. I try to go every year.

If I really want to get into the fun, I put on a red shirt and groom my beard. Most crafters are garrulous by nature, and I am constantly greeted with, "Hi, Santa!" The shoppers are usually more surprised than the crafters to see me and often do double takes. Many smile broadly and nod in recognition. Some greet me with comments like, "Where are your reindeer?" or "How are things going at the Pole?"

Of course these questions are not new to me, and I'm always well prepared. "The reindeer are at the North Pole; it is much too hot here for them this time of year." Or "Things are going great at the North Pole. Pete, the chief elf, is in charge. We did have a slight slowdown on the Barbie line yesterday, but today we're back to full production."

Of course there is always someone who asks, "Has anyone ever told you that you look like Santa Claus?"

∼✺∽

I have already introduced Pete, the patriarch of a family of little people who "elf" for me every night at Stone Mountain Park. He sits beside me in his little chair, and we keep a running dialogue going between kids. His interaction with the kids and families is fun for me to watch. He is also receptionist at my ministry, Friends of Disabled Adults and Children, Inc.

Many families tell us they have been coming for ten or fifteen years. Pete's usual response is, "Wow, I was just a little guy back then, wasn't I?" Most times folks don't know how to respond to that, since he is only three feet nine inches tall and has been that size for fifty years. Pete loves it.

His wife, Mary Alice, and his children, Bunny, Heidi, and Trent, have also elfed for me from time to time. They are all a delightful bunch. At least once a year they plan a trip to the Park with some of their friends and their friends' children, all little people. The "big people" there usually can't believe their eyes. We all have a lot of fun together, but I'll talk more about that later.

## Typical Encounters

I love those encounters that happen in public places when I least expect them. For instance, I was eating at a

Golden Corral restaurant in Marietta, Georgia. We were having a spirited evening. The couple with me had not met me before that night and seemed intrigued with the whole Santa persona. I was wearing black trousers and a red knit shirt, and when I went to the buffet, the couple followed along behind me and watched how people reacted to having Santa in their midst.

We were in the middle of our meal when I felt a tap on my left shoulder. I turned to see a beautiful little girl of about six. She was wide-eyed, with a hesitant, apprehensive look on her face. I smiled and said, "Hello, Sweetie, how are you?"

She ignored my question and blurted out what she had come to ask: "Are you Santa Claus?"

(I have told you about such a conversation before, but I enjoy it, so let me repeat.)

"No, Sweetie, I am the Easter Bunny."

"No, you aren't! You don't look like the Easter Bunny." She said this so forcefully that I knew I was not toying with just any little girl. This was a smart kid, and I had better be on my toes.

"Oh, who do I look like?"

"You look like Santa Claus!"

Leaning forward, I raised my finger to my lips and said, "Shhh, don't tell anybody. It has to be a secret, okay?"

She raised her finger to her lips and, mimicking me, said in a near whisper, "Shhh, okay. I won't tell anybody." The expression on her face was so cute, it took my breath away. She leaned toward me and said, "Can I tell my mom?" I nodded okay, and she took off to a table in the corner. Halfway across the restaurant, she shouted, "It is Santa Claus, Mom! I told you it was!"

In a few minutes she was back with another tap on my shoulder. "Where are your reindeer?"

"They're at the North Pole. It's much too warm here for reindeer today."

A quick nod and she was gone again.

She returned shortly. "Do you know what I want for Christmas?"

"No, I don't. Why don't you tell me?"

She elbowed her way between me and my friend, and when I slid my chair back, she pushed her way onto my lap. (She clearly knew she had to be on my lap to give me her order.) As she climbed up, she began to give me her list. It started, in typical little-girl fashion, with Barbies and a Baby Alive doll. Then she threw in an iPod, Mp3 player, Xbox, Game Boy, Nintendo DS, and a couple of other electronic games. She finished up with a cell phone. Boy, she really was a sophisticated little girl. But these items could force her family into bankruptcy! I told her she had a big list and that I would see what I could do about it, but not to count on all of that. She said she knew she wouldn't get it all.

This time when she ran back to her mom, I watched where she went. I discovered that her mother was a waitress in the restaurant, and I wondered what kind of life they led. I found myself wishing I could just hand her a Game Boy or something, but my pockets were empty. All I had in there were some suckers and a couple of Matchbox cars.

The place where I hold forth most of the season is the throne at Stone Mountain Park. They move me around from year to year, from building to building, but the scene on the throne itself is almost always the same. One year they did make it more difficult than usual. The throne had a backdrop of four red bookcases that were filled with toys of all kinds. When I asked the kids what they wanted for Christmas, they spent a lot of time telling me the toys on the shelves were what their little hearts desired. Some even went so far as to say they wanted a red car or a yellow truck, both of which were prominently displayed. But at least I didn't have to sit there while they were trying to think of something to say. That is when I discovered that very few of the kids come ready to spout off a well-thought-out list of things they actually do want. Many times, when I ask the question, there is no answer at all—just a long pause as their minds go blank.

But sometimes the answers do give me something to report to you.

And sometimes the answers will break your heart.

One special girl's story comes to mind. She looked like any of the thousands of kids who had sat on my lap. She was about seven, which is older than some. She was pleasant enough as I asked her how she was doing. But when I asked, "What would you like for Christmas?" a dark cloud came over her face.

Immediately she responded, "All I want is for my family to be together for Christmas."

"And what would that take?" I asked.

"You have to get my mama out of jail."

The air went out of me involuntarily. But throwing caution to the wind, I decided to go on and ask, "Where is your dad?"

This time she sighed, "We don't know. He's been gone a long time."

"Well, who is taking care of you?" I felt so helpless.

"I'm living with my grandma; that's her over there." A lovely lady waved as the girl pointed to her. I could

More Pages from the Red Suit Diaries

not even begin to fathom the pain her grandma must have been feeling.

"Well, Sweetie, how about we pray for your mama and your daddy?"

"Now?"

"Sure, right now." And we did. I threw in a prayer for Grandma too.

After I said amen, I gave her a big hug and told her, "Don't ever forget that God loves you, and Santa loves you too." And that was the absolute truth.

❦

I have had several kids who told me that they wanted their dads to come home from Iraq. But I was not prepared for another little girl who told me she wanted her daddy *and* her mommy to come home.

"Both of them?" I blurted out.

"Yeah," she answered. "They're both in the National Guard and they both got called up. I am staying with my mom's sister and her kids."

"Are you all getting along?" Dumb question, Santa!

"Yeah, we are. It's kind of like going to your cousins' for a visit. I like visiting my cousins, but it's been so long! I miss my mom and dad. I email them every day and tell them what's going on, but . . . I do miss them."

"Of course you miss them. I know they're proud of you for being such a good girl about it and I'm sure they're looking forward to your being together again."

There was no dark cloud here, just a powerful, good feeling about the whole situation. I am sure that was because of the sensitivity of her aunt and cousins and the encouragement of her parents, who weren't there in body but certainly were in heart.

There are times at the Park when I am not swamped with kids. I talk to Pete, or the elf on duty, and try to stay alert, but that doesn't always work. Usually I have been busy during the day and am pretty tired by the time I get to the Park. The four hours in the evening when I'm on duty can drag on if there aren't a lot of kids. I may as well admit it. Sometimes I nod off while I'm waiting for the next kid! It is usually for just a moment, but on a couple of occasions, I have really enjoyed some deep, REM sleep.

One time I was sound asleep when I felt a hand shaking my knee. I didn't move but soon I heard a little boy's voice say, "Santa." A moment later the shaking grew more vigorous and the voice more strident. "*Santa!*"

I kept my head down and said, loud enough for him and Pete to hear, "Amen." Then I raised my head and did a normal, routine interview.

Afterwards, Pete said, "I can't believe you pulled that one off."

I just couldn't let anyone think Santa was so bored he went to sleep on the throne!

❧

Sometimes, just when I'm beginning to think I have heard about everything I will ever hear from kids, I am caught off guard again.

One little guy looked completely average. He was about six, blond, and very outgoing. He answered my first question with elaborate enthusiasm, "I am fine, doing good, being a good boy."

I noticed that his mother had approached closer than parents usually do. I motioned her back a little to get her out of the way of the photographer; then as soon as the camera flashed, she moved in close again.

"Well then, what do you want for Christmas?"

This is the part that practically knocked me off the throne. He said, with that same enthusiasm, "I want a ghost!"

"Whoa, wait a minute," I responded. "Did you say you want a ghost?"

"Yeah, a ghost. That's all I want, a ghost."

I looked at Mom, and she was nodding.

"A ghost?" I asked her.

The little guy hopped off my lap and took off for the craft area. His job was done. He had told me what he wanted.

Mom stepped up and said, "That's all he's talked about since he saw a movie a few months ago. He thinks a ghost will keep him company, help with his homework, and do all his chores."

"Well, good luck handling that one!" I said.

"Yeah, thanks," she said over her shoulder as she moved toward the picture-ordering counter.

A ghost, of all things. Good grief!

It is funny how closely kids are paying attention and yet how much they miss. One little fellow was about five and all business. He prefaced his list by saying, "At my mom's house I want you to bring . . ." and he continued with several items.

When he had finished, I asked him, "And what do you want at your dad's house?"

"Oh yeah, thanks," he answered and then launched into a new list with different items. Then he said, "Okay, that's all." He hopped off my lap and was gone to his mom. They moved away to the craft area, and a few moments later, Mom stepped up to me.

"How did you do that?" she asked.

"Do what?" I responded, completely puzzled by her query.

"My son just told me that you had to be the real Santa because you knew that his dad and I were divorced. How did you know that?"

I tapped my forehead with my forefinger and asked, "Why are you surprised? You know I know everything."

She smiled, paused a moment, and then walked away.

That was no great magic. I was just listening and following the clues.

Another mother stepped up to me after her five-year-old had finished giving me his list and had moved off to his dad. She told me her older son could not make it that night but that he wanted her to give me his list because he was absolutely convinced I was the real Santa. I asked her why he was so convinced.

She said that the previous year he could not be there either, and he had told his little brother to tell me he wanted a hunting bow for Christmas. The little brother had done it and told his mom about it on the way home. That was the first time she had heard about a hunting bow. She talked to Dad, and they decided he was mature enough to be trusted with one. So on Christmas morning, he got his bow.

He was ecstatic. He asked the family, "How did Santa know I wanted a bow?"

His little brother said, "I told him you wanted one, like you told me to do."

Later the big brother told his mom and dad, "I knew that Santa at Stone Mountain was the real one."

"And he made sure his friends heard the story too," Mom said as she left.

I absolutely love doing the unexpected!

I noticed a particular mom and daughter communicating in American Sign Language (ASL) while they were waiting. I couldn't tell which one of them was deaf, but I thought it was the daughter—a young lady of about eight or nine.

As they were approaching the throne, I did the ASL for "I sign." Both their faces lit up. Maybe they were both deaf.

I seated the daughter on my lap and signed, "Are you a good girl?"

She nodded vigorously.

Then I signed, "What do you want for Christmas?"

I know the signs for some toys, but she was flying through her list so fast I was barely able to keep up. Then she finished her list and gave me a big hug. As she started to move away, she looked over her shoulder and said, "Thanks, Santa."

Then her mother rushed up to me, hugged my neck, and kissed me on the cheek. It was the mother who was deaf, and the girl had wanted her mom to know what she was asking for. I was so glad I had the ability to make that happen.

Here's a funny one. I had heard from somebody that some kids really do like to work in the yard. Mine certainly never did, so I had a hard time believing it.

This kid looked like an ordinary six-year-old. When I asked him what he wanted for Christmas, I expected to hear an iPod, Mp3 player, or Nintendo DS like all the other boys his age I'd seen so far. But no. His response was, "A leaf blower!"

"A leaf blower?" I responded.

"No, make that two leaf blowers," he answered.

"Two leaf blowers!" I was even more amazed.

"Yeah," he responded, quite matter-of-factly. "One for me and one for my brother so we can work in the yard at the same time."

"Of course, how silly of me!" I responded, chuckling. I looked at mom and shrugged my shoulders.

She stepped forward and said, "That's the only thing he's talked about getting for months."

"Does he really work in the yard?" I inquired.

"Yes, he does. They both love to work in the yard. They would rather work outside than play outside."

"Wow, that's really something. Want to trade them?"

A smile, but no answer. It was worth a try, anyway.

People do ascribe a lot of magical powers to Santa Claus, but he definitely has his limits. One little boy's demeanor made me think something was troubling him. He was less than exuberant as he walked to the throne and got up on my lap.

Instead of asking what he wanted for Christmas, I almost asked him what was bothering him. But before I could say anything to him, he said, "There is only one thing I want for Christmas this year, Santa."

"And what would that be?" I asked.

"All I want is for my brother's diabetes to be cured. He doesn't deserve that."

"No, he doesn't deserve that." I answered. "Nobody deserves something like that. Nobody. But bad things do happen to good people, and there is no explanation for that. One thing we can do is pray for him. Let's do that now."

My prayer was for the brother and for this little boy who loved him enough to give up his Christmas for him. Then I promised I would pray some more for both of them. I encouraged him to pray for his brother too, and turned him loose. As he went away, his steps seemed a bit jauntier. I did not reveal to him that I'm a diabetic too.

ക്ക

Another kid looked skeptical as he walked toward my throne. His arms were folded across his chest and he seemed apprehensive. He stepped onto my stool and swung onto my left leg.

"My mama made me come here for a picture," he blurted. "I don't believe in you."

"Oh, you don't? Why don't you believe in me?"

"You got on a phony beard, that's why!"

Now I do work hard to make my beard look well groomed, but I had never had anyone *tell* me it was phony. And besides, he hadn't really looked at it closely. I decided to take the kind approach. "Well, have you really looked at it?" I asked. At least he hadn't tried to snatch it off like a couple of kids have.

He turned and looked at my face. He jumped perceptibly, and his face took on a new look. He turned his head back and forth as he looked, and then he almost shouted, "Wait, it really is growing right out of your face!"

I said, "Sure it is. That's what real beards do. They grow right out of your face."

This time he really did shout, "It *is* real! It's a *real beard*! He's the *real* Santa!" Then he jumped off my lap, but as he started to walk away, he whirled around and leaned toward me. "Now I do believe," he said confidentially. Then he walked away. A little while later, he came back and handed me his list without a word, just a big grin on his face.

I have always been something of a car nut, but I did not know that young kids can be car nuts too.

This little fellow had bright, excited eyes as he climbed onto my lap. I didn't even have a chance to ask him my questions. Immediately he launched into his list by saying, "I want cars, lots of them. I want a big race car set, a bunch of Matchbox cars, some remote control cars, and some NASCAR collectible race cars."

More Pages from the Red Suit Diaries

"Just cars, huh?" I finally got a word in.

"Yeah, and lots of them," he responded as he hopped down and walked away.

⟡

Another little guy had some real specifics in mind when he put in his requests. I should have had a clue when he came up wearing a Dale Earnhardt Jr. jacket and a Mark Martin baseball cap.

"I want only model NASCAR race cars. I already have some, but I want the rest of them, all in one-to-eighteen scale."

"Who do you already have?" I asked, trying to be helpful.

"Well, let's see," he mused. "I already have Dale Junior, Mark Martin (*why did I know that already?*), Kyle Petty, Kasey Kahne," and he went on to name several more. When he stopped with familiar names, he added, "There are some rookies coming along that don't have model cars out yet, but when they do come out, I want them."

Here was a man who was clearly devoted to his

hobby. I couldn't help but wonder if he had caught that obsession from his parents. Things like that are often contagious. I looked into the crowd of observers, and sure enough, there was a couple who had on Dale Earnhardt Jr. jackets. Dad even had on a Mark Martin cap. Must run in the family, I guess!

Kids can sometimes get very specific, like one young lady who wanted to make sure I knew her name was Andie. She even spelled it out carefully so I would know it was not spelled like a boy's name.

Her first request was for some animals from the Littlest Pet Shop collection. She made sure I knew that part; then she gave me a list of animals: a dog, a cat, a kitten, a monkey, and several others. When she finished, she said, "Okay, got that?"

I nodded, and she went on.

"I want a train set with wooden tracks."

I nodded and said, "Like Thomas the Tank Engine trains?"

"Yeah," she brightened up even more and went on

to name several of the Thomas characters. "Make sure you include some bridges and trestles and buildings with the set, okay?"

She went on, "I want a big Fairytopia, a big one, not a little one. Okay?"

I nodded again. I was not familiar with that one. This was the first request for it, so I made a mental note to check it out in the toy catalog.

I was getting curious about how long this could go on.

"I want a butterfly doll set in pink. Got it?"

"Got it." I responded.

"And the last thing is . . .

*Finally, the end is in sight,* I thought.

"I want a Dorothy wig from *The Wizard of Oz.*"

"So you want to look like Dorothy, huh?"

"Yeah, she is so cute!"

"Yes she is. Well, that is quite a specific list, and I will see what I can do to find all those things."

"Okay. Thank you," she said merrily and ran to her parents.

Another guy had an obsession with motor vehicles. He told me, "I want some toy trucks. Lots of them. All kinds and sizes and colors."

"How many of them do you want?" I was searching for specifics.

"I want five hundred of them," he said, "all sizes and colors and kinds of trucks."

"Is that all you want?" I queried.

"Yep, just trucks." Then he jumped off my lap.

He took two steps and turned around just as I was helping a little girl up and said, "On second thought, don't make it that many. My dad can't count that high."

Sometimes some of the results of sibling conflict become visible even to a casual observer. I remember a little guy who looked like a fighter as he mounted my knee. As I helped him up, I felt a cast on his forearm. Checking it out, I found it went all the way up to his armpit. I asked him, "How did you break your arm?"

He answered, "My brother did it."

"What did he hit you with?" I asked.

"A baseball bat."

"A baseball bat! My goodness. Well, should I put him on the bad boy list?"

"No," he answered enthusiastically. "He didn't mean to. It was an accident. He was aiming at my head. I put my arm up and he hit that instead."

I saw another case of sibling conflict at the Atlanta RV show. I was touring through several Class A RVs parked outside and was followed on board a very nice unit by a mother and her brood of four boys. The oldest boy, about fourteen, came on right behind me and sat down in the driver's seat. His next brother came on and sat in the passenger seat. Mom came on next. She was well in when the third son, about eight or ten, came up the steps.

This unit had the entry door right in front of the passenger seat. As the third boy went by his brother, the older boy stuck out his leg and tripped the younger one, sending him sprawling to the floor. I was looking right at them.

Their mother was looking at the kitchen of the RV, but when she heard the noise, she turned around.

I said loudly, "I don't believe he did that—and right in front of me too!" I reached into my back pocket for my day planner and opened it up. "I think he needs to go on my bad boy list for that little trick."

Mom nodded to me.

"Oh, rats! I've lost my pen," I exclaimed.

Mom said, "I have one," and instantly handed me the one in her hand.

I took it and asked her his name.

"It's Dillon, Santa. You should remember him."

"Oh, yes, I do. Let me make a note of this to add to his record." I wrote down a few words and handed the pen back to Mom. I thanked her and went on to finish my tour of the RV.

About a half hour later, in another part of the exhibit area, I saw the boys again. "Hello, Dillon," I said.

"I hope you're being a good boy now." He nodded through a sheepish grin.

## Other Encounters

I hate shopping. I have always hated shopping. When I need something, I usually know exactly what it is, go to the store, buy it, and leave. And now, with my beard, shopping has gotten extremely difficult. Actually, I don't mind the Santa encounters. I truly enjoy them, but they do complicate the shopping that I already dread.

Let me describe my typical shopping trip by explaining the one I had just yesterday. I made sure I was not wearing any red clothes. I had on a green shirt, brown jacket, blue FODAC baseball cap, black pants, and brown shoes. As I walked in the door the greeter immediately said, "Hello, Santa, welcome to Wal-Mart. Here is a cart for you and our latest ad. Toys are to your left in the far corner of the store."

I smiled, said hello, waited while she finished her spiel, took the cart, and started toward the housewares department. I had gone only about fifty feet when I heard someone behind me say, "Ho, ho, ho! Hello, Santa."

I turned and a large man with a scraggly salt-and-pepper goatee was standing by his cart, smiling at me. I smiled back, and he said, "You have a lovely beard."

I said, "You could have one too, if you quit trimming that fuzz on your face and let it grow on out."

He said, "I tried that once and it drove me crazy. How can you stand it?"

"I never think about it." I answered. "It's just part of me, and I never mess with it."

"Well, it sure does look good. You look like the real Santa."

"Thank you very much," I said and meant every word of it.

I had almost made it to the housewares area when a manager came by and said, "Finding everything you're looking for, Santa?"

He helped me locate the storage tubs I had come for.

I pushed my cart up to the checkout counter. The cashier looked up and said dryly, "Hello, Santa. Did you find everything you were looking for?"

"Yes, sure did," I answered, as she rang up the sale.

On my way out, the door hadn't even shut when I heard two small voices saying, "Hi, Santa! Hi, Santa! Hi, Santa!" I saw two little guys of about eight or ten and gave them high fives as they went into the store with their mom.

Is that a typical shopping trip? Yeah, pretty much.

Here's another version. I was at Sam's Club and saw an older lady in an electric wheelchair. Her left leg was missing from above the knee. When I got close enough, I could see that the chair had come from FODAC. It had one of our stickers on it—from at least eight years ago. There was a rush of pride and gratitude that God had used me and our ministry to help this lady. Our paths crossed a few times as we moved around the store, and finally, I could stand it no longer. "How is that chair running these days, Ma'am?"

"Good," she answered. "It's running real good, always has."

"How long have you had it?"

"Ten years. My son and I were just talking about that," she said, motioning to a younger man who was accompanying her.

"Oh, yeah," he interjected. "You're the Santa from the wheelchair place, aren't you?"

"Yes, I am." I answered, "How did you know?"

"I've seen you on television and read about you in the paper."

"So your mama's chair is still working okay?"

"Yes," he answered. "She uses it all the time, and it just keeps on going."

"I'm glad to hear that. And I'm glad that the Lord used us to help her through a difficult time."

"Well, you sure did that," he responded enthusiastically. "That chair has made a big difference in her life. Thank you so much for your help."

"You are certainly welcome. God bless you," I responded as I moved on.

I have done Santa at that store for the employees'
children, and when I got to the checkout, the clerk
said, "Hey, Santa, how's it going?"

"Great!" I answered. "Absolutely supreme!" And
I meant it.

# *the greatest of these is love*

## My Childhood Santa Visits

People seem fascinated by how I came to look like this and portray the jolly fat guy. It does seem an unlikely outcome for a man who has been through all that I have. But it is not all that surprising when you consider my roots.

My mama was a wonderfully kind, loving person, and she did all she could to keep my brother Peter and me believing in Santa for as long as possible. My earliest memories are of making construction paper chains and popcorn strings to decorate our Christmas tree. We hung anything we could find that was colorful on the tree and put those chains all around them. We didn't have lights, and Mama resisted our pleas to put real candles on the tree.

She would buy fruit and we would hang apples, oranges, and tangerines (my favorite). We would watch the fruit carefully. If one began to look overripe, we would take it off the tree and eat it.

We always had a natural tree that was cut off our own, or an unsuspecting neighbor's, property. My brother Robert, seven years older than me, was in charge of fetching the tree. He always chose a cedar variety. I loved the smell of that cedar in the house, and we kept it up so long that sometimes it looked like the pine beetle had its way with it before we finally took down its scrawny skeleton.

Mama never knew exactly where the tree came from, but Peter and I knew every tree and bush on our seven acres—and most of the ones on our neighbor's property. We never told Mama where we got the tree, because if it came from our neighbor's property, she would have had a fit, even though it was purloined in the pursuit of holiday cheer.

It was not until I was about ten that Robert finally let me go along on the hunt for the perfect tree. He had his eye on a grand specimen that was growing beside a pond on the Causey family farm, more than

More Pages from the Red Suit Diaries

a mile from our house. We took an axe and a bow saw and made our way through the woods to the spot. The tree was located about halfway between the wood line and the pond and sat in an open clearing. It was at least twelve feet tall. We wanted only the top eight feet, so Robert outlined the plan to me as we stood in the shadow of the woods.

He would run out to the tree with the axe and chop the thing down. As soon as it toppled over, my job was to run out with the bow saw and cut it off at the designated spot. Then he would drop the axe, grab the tree, and run for the woods. I would pick up the axe and the saw and hightail it for the woods myself. There was only one complication. Mr. Causey had a reputation for protecting his property with a rifle!

At the given signal, Robert ran to the tree and began chopping. At the third lick, the shooting began. We had agreed that we didn't think Causey would intend to shoot us, and we were well over a hundred yards away from his house. But I was concerned that in trying to miss us, he could do some damage.

At the sound of the first shot, Robert began chopping frantically. In a moment, over she went. I dashed out with the bow saw and was whipping that thing back and forth so fast I thought it would turn red hot. Robert's frenzied yelling for me to hurry up didn't help my nerves any more than the fusillade of gunfire.

The moment the trunk was severed, Robert snatched up the tree and dashed for the wood line. I picked up the axe and was right behind him. We ran on into the woods a good distance before the sound of rifle fire stopped. On the way home we figured that Causey would be in our backyard waiting for us, so we made our way carefully to determine if the coast was clear before delivering our bounty.

It was. We strolled casually into the yard after we had put the tools in the barn and nailed the crossbar stand to the bottom of the tree. We placed the tree in the customary spot in the living room as Mama made her usual exclamations of pleasure. We never did hear a word from Causey, and we never again violated his property line for any reason.

As an aside, I later spent twenty years in the Marine Corps as an infantry officer. I still believe I was shot at more times that day on Causey's property than during all those years of being a professional target.

～❦～

Our mama never threatened us with retribution from Santa if we didn't behave. She believed so strongly in the innate human quality of love, and the power of God's love, that she just wanted us to feel it and never wanted to take credit for it. Santa was a way she could show God's love to us through an anonymous third party.

Peter and I still talk about the night we actually saw Santa Claus. Mama always insisted we go to bed early on Christmas Eve, and we always fought sleep for several hours before we would drift off. But this one night was almost balmy, and we decided we would climb out the window of our room onto the front porch roof and wait to see Santa make his appearance.

We took our blankets along and wrapped ourselves in them. It was a breathlessly beautiful night with clear skies, millions of stars, and a near-full moon. It was just like a night earlier that year when we had sat out there to watch the Perseid meteor shower. That had been October 9, Peter's birthday, and it was one spectacular sight.

On Christmas Eve there was a hush over the land. That far out in the country, there was no ambient noise at all. We talked in whispers. We heard the Pringles' horse whinny in the barn across the fields. Then, suddenly, we nearly jumped out of our skins. There was the faint sound of sleigh bells somewhere in the distance. It could have been a mile, maybe even two miles away, but it was the sound of sleigh bells for sure. Then we thought we saw an object moving through the sky. Slowly, magically, it moved directly across the face of the bright near-full moon! It looked like . . . it could only be . . . it had to be! It couldn't be anything or anyone else!

We grabbed our blankets, scrambled back into our room, and closed the window, locking it tight. Jumping into bed, we covered up our heads and huddled

More Pages from the Red Suit Diaries

together, not knowing whether we were scared to death or excited with anticipation. In moments, we were asleep.

Neither of us can remember the gifts we received the next morning, but we will both go to our graves convinced that on that magical, star-filled night, we saw the man!

That does not mean that there weren't some times our faith was called into question, like late on Christmas Eve the year that I was ten. We had been shopping all day, and Peter and I had been sent on several meaningless errands so Mama and Daddy could make their secret purchases. Peter and I went along with it since we knew we were to be the beneficiaries of this subterfuge. Daddy made several treks to the car with packages, and we were dying to look into those mysterious bundles, but knew better than to let on that we even knew about them, much less cared what was inside.

If I knew anything back then, it was the feeling of the backseat of our old '37 Chevrolet. I had sat in every conceivable position on it, and I had lain down to sleep there many times during the bumpy six-mile ride down the dirt road to our house. This night, it felt different. There seemed to be a new bump in the seat.

I slid my hand behind the seat cushion and discovered a box under there. It felt about three inches thick, ten inches wide, and longer than I could reach in one direction. I found an open edge and eased my hand inside the box. Immediately I recognized the shape and feel. It was the bolt handle of a rifle. Now that was exciting! I didn't think the rifle was for me, at my tender age, so I figured it must be for Robert.

The next morning, as we were unwrapping gifts, I kept watching for the long box. Finally, when all the gifts had been unwrapped, Mama told Robert to check behind the tree in the corner to see if there was anything left. Sure enough (surprise, surprise!), he pulled out a .22-caliber, single-shot rifle.

He became an expert shot very quickly and earned a reputation as a one-shot hunter. A bigger surprise was that Mama proved to be a better shooter than her son. One of her favorite tricks was to lay a Coke bottle on its side, then shoot through the neck of the bottle and blow out the bottom. She could also shoot well on the fly. We could toss a tin can into the air, and she could hit it about every time; she could also shoot it straight from the hip.

But I digress. Back to Christmas!

Mama persisted in her commitment to keep Christmas and Santa alive for us. We always opened gifts on Christmas morning, never on Christmas Eve. Even when I came home from college, we continued the ritual. There were always some gifts from Santa that she had slipped under the tree after we had gone to bed.

When I brought my own kids home years later, she insisted that if they wanted to open gifts at her house, it had to be done on Christmas morning. My kids loved it as much as I did.

Maybe it was her persistence and her unwavering belief in the power of love that kept Christmas alive for me through all those years.

When I left the Marine Corps and stopped shaving, my beard grew out mostly white. This helped my transition to the Red Suit. I think Santa was always down deep inside there somewhere. My white beard just helped him come to the surface.

## The Johnston Family

I promised I'd talk some more about the family of little people who play the role of elves at Stone Mountain Park. I want you to know what an incredible group of people they are.

Pete is the patriarch. He comes from a family of eleven children and is the only little person in the bunch. His folks were farmers in Tifton, Georgia, and he learned early to work hard at whatever job he undertook. He withstood a lot of ribbing and kidding from his family and friends in school, and rather than becoming embittered and angry about being "different," he developed a wonderful sense of humor. It's clear that Pete is quite comfortable with the person he is.

Pete has been my elf most frequently, and we have become very close. He is a year older than I am, and we relate well with each other. We keep a running commentary about the visitors and the kids' requests all evening long. Pete has a warm, loving spirit about him.

Several years ago Pete got laid off after a company merger, and he found himself idle for the first time in almost thirty years. His wife, Mary Alice, asked if I had any job openings at FODAC for him. I didn't have one, but I made one. Pete is now the first person people see when they come to our building. He is the receptionist, customer service representative, and telephone operator and does a wonderful job of keeping all those responsibilities straight. He is extremely organized and completely unflappable—the perfect person for the position.

Like many little people, Pete has some orthopedic problems and has had surgery on his hips and back. Fortunately, neither of his jobs requires him to be nimble and quick. His sweet disposition keeps him popular with the Santa visitors and the folks who come to FODAC for help.

Mary Alice is the matriarch (and, according to Pete, the boss) of the family. She was also raised in a loving, fun-filled family in DeKalb County, Georgia. Even as a child she wanted to be a teacher. For the past thirty-one years, she has realized that dream as a kindergarten teacher in the Henry County school system. Anytime she is elfing at the Park, someone will recognize her and greet her like a long-lost relative. I guess in a sense, she is a relative to the many people whose lives she's touched.

Her favorite thing about elfing is the adoring, completely trusting look most kids bring to the throne. It is a look she sees often herself, I would think, but she says there is something different about seeing it in the Santa setting.

Sometimes her two worlds run together. Occasionally a kid from her class will come to see Santa while she is the elf. Sometimes questions arise later. One day at school, a little boy demanded to know what

More Pages from the Red Suit Diaries

was going on. She told him that she was also a teacher at the North Pole. He was freaked out that even the elves have to go to school. She assured him that people are going to school of some sort most of their lives to learn new things about their jobs or even to change professions. He didn't like that idea one bit!

Mary Alice did find out that the power of Santa works, even when the big guy is not around. One year she and her son Trent went to the Atlanta Farmer's Market to shop for a Christmas tree. Leaning out of the car, she asked one vendor if he had a special price for Santa and his elves. He laughed and said, "Sure, if he comes to get it himself."

Mary Alice said, "He couldn't come himself, but he sent us." Then she and Trent hopped out of the car.

The guy was completely taken aback when he saw them and said, "Well, I guess I do have a special price for y'all!" He marked down their chosen tree by 50 percent.

Sometimes at school, to get some order in her class, Mary Alice tells boisterous kids that she knows Santa.

Then one day one of her students actually saw her with me at the Park. She told him, "I told you I knew Santa, didn't I?" By the time school started the next day, every kid in the class knew that Mrs. Johnston was a personal friend of Santa Claus!

Heidi was the very first Johnston family elf I met, on the very first evening I arrived at Stone Mountain Park in 1991. I had been told there would be some little people there portraying elves, but in the excitement of the day, I had completely forgotten.

When I walked through the crowd outside the train station and went into the chicken restaurant where I would be working, there was Heidi. I was just greeting her when Trent walked up. I was meeting these folks for the first time, but the crowd watching would assume that I knew them very well. We agreed that we would get to know each other as the evening wore on.

Heidi was eighteen and a senior in high school. Trent was fifteen and a sophomore. Immediately I was impressed by the wonderful personalities and delightful sense of humor these two had. They seemed very mature for their ages. In fact, they had been elfing longer than I had been Clausing, and I learned a lot from them on that first shift—and much more over the years. It was my distinct pleasure to watch these two grow up.

Heidi went away to college and became a nurse. One year she brought by a handsome young man to help her elf. She introduced him as Barry, her boyfriend. A year later she returned with something sparkly on her hand. She and Barry were engaged. He had passed his CPA exam, and wedding plans were well underway. I reminded her that I am an ordained minister, and before the evening was over, I had it all planned. We would have the wedding party and all the guests in their elfing outfits, if appropriate, and Santa in his Red Suit. It would be tons of fun—and the media would love it.

The following Christmas, Heidi showed me her left hand again, and there was a wedding band to complement the diamond. Rats! She had gone ahead without me. But I was thrilled for the two of them and very excited about their future.

The next year I heard that Heidi was pregnant, and soon another granddaughter was born into the Johnston family. This little girl was going to be a regular-sized person. Her name is Carrigan, and she was fortunate to inherit her parents' beauty genes. As is the nature of things, she was taller than her parents by age nine. Heidi's mothering and work duties eventually led her away from elfing, but she remains a favorite of mine.

Trent grew up too. During my second year at the Park, he decided he didn't want to go to college. He had already proven to me that he was an intelligent, energetic, industrious young man, and I knew he would do well at anything he attempted. The most impressive thing he has done is to create a remarkable family. He met Amber at a national meeting of the Little People of America in Chicago when they were both eighteen. They knew immediately that they wanted to be married but waited until they were twenty.

I met Amber at a Little People of America convention in Atlanta in 1997. She is a tiny lady with a huge heart. It was quite a sight to see her five years later when she was eight months pregnant. She looked like a basketball with legs, arms, and a head. She delivered a beautiful little guy they named Jonah. A couple of years later, his sister Elizabeth joined the family. She would be a little person too. The doctor recommended that there be no more babies because Amber was so small, but that did not mean they couldn't add to their family. A year later Trent and Amber heard about a girl in an orphanage—a little person. Life looked grim for her in Russia, as it was very unlikely that she would ever be adopted. Trent and Amber decided immediately that they would be her new parents.

In Russia bureaucratic red tape caused delay after delay, but they were determined that they would not go home without this child. One week stretched into three, and Trent and Amber persisted until the officials finally relented and let them go home together.

Anna's age put her right in between Jonah and Elizabeth, and she looked like she could be a blood sibling to them. It took her about two minutes to fit into the family, and with three kids under four years old, life was fun for all.

Like many young children, they were all terrified of Santa. The fact that their "Poppi," Pete, was an elf for Santa did not impress them. They were not coming anywhere near me. It would take a dramatic lesson in 2005, during the FODAC Breakfast-with-Santa fundraiser, to get them past that.

The breakfast is held annually at the Marriott Evergreen Conference Center and Resort at Stone Mountain Park. Every year it has grown in size and financial impact for FODAC.

It is a huge kick for me to walk into a room of 250 people who are attending the breakfast and watch them react to my sudden appearance in the doorway. Pete brings some of his kids, their spouses, and their kids, and they all help pass out the few hundred toys we have accumulated for this event.

In 2005 Pete and his family decided it was time for seven-year-old Jonah to become an official elf. Amber fixed him an elf outfit, and he was very excited to be a real helper for Santa. And help he did. He was a bit shy at first, but soon he was dashing around among the presents, picking out special ones for each kid that came to my lap. Soon it was his turn to climb onto my lap, which he did without a moment's hesitation.

After that morning, he went home and told his sisters about it. A few days later when they came to the Park, they were all over me too. At the 2006 breakfast they were all elves, and what a wonderful sight that was!

And there was a new member of the family that year. Trent and Amber had heard about a baby in a Korean orphanage that was a little person and, with a lot less bureaucratic wrangling than when Anna was adopted, Alex joined the family. Amber has proven to be a wonderful mother, and Mary Alice is an apt mentor for her. It is such a wonderful thing to watch the whole family interacting with these active, energetic kids.

Throw in Heidi's Carrington and Bunny's daughter Halle—who is regular size—and the whole house fills up very quickly with love and laughter. Sitting and watching, one would wonder why all families can't be like this, simply loving one another.

Trent has a few favorite memories of elfing. One is the time he noticed the little girl on my lap had her shoes on the wrong feet. He pointed that out to me, and I said to her, "You have your shoes on the wrong feet, Sweetie."

She looked down for a moment, then looked back up with a frown. She said, "These are the only feet that I have!"

But one of Trent's most favorite stories is the night a young couple came to sit on my lap. As I always do, I asked if they were dating. They said yes, so I told them to hold hands for the photo.

After it was taken, the young man continued to hold his girl's hand. He said, "I have chosen this time and this place to ask this question."

Trent and I both heard his comment and knew something was about to happen. Trent jumped off his stool beside me and ran around in front so he could see their faces.

The man pulled his arm from behind me and with an obviously practiced move, popped open a little black box. "I love you with all my heart," he said. "Will you marry me?"

Wow, I thought. A proposal, right here on my lap! How neat!

He had caught his girlfriend completely off guard. She paused for a long time, then looked again at the ring and blurted out, "What, are you kidding me? No way! Never! Forget it!" She jumped off my lap and nearly knocked Trent over on her way to the door.

The guy just sat there in shock.

In a moment I said, "Don't just sit here, boy. Go get her!" He jumped up and took off after her.

I don't know the rest of the story, but I did share it with another young couple who came to have their picture taken on Santa's lap. The next Christmas they returned—and showed me their wedding rings. They had come back to the Park that spring for the Laser Show, and at the height of the fireworks, he had asked her to marry him. She had, of course, said yes.

Pete and Mary Alice's daughter Bunny is another wonderful mother and dynamic person. She's also a great elf. I get the impression that nothing is going to stand in the way of this dynamo. She is a real go-getter. One night, during a lull in the action, she decided to go get a cup of hot chocolate. On her way back, she stepped up on the stage and tripped over the edge of a rug in front of the throne. She came crashing down on her belly, right in front of the throne. I shouted and jumped up to help her. But before I could lift a finger, she went crawling across the floor to retrieve her cup of hot chocolate (still safe under the lid), which had rolled away from her. She set it upright and then jumped up on her own. She picked up her cup, sat back down in her chair, and brushed off my expressions of concern. "I fall all the time," she said, sipping her treasured drink.

Bunny likes to work the line some too. I have seen her standing right up against a reluctant visitor, lecturing him and shaking her finger in his face, which she has to reach up to get to. Now she is a supervisor in an office, and I know I wouldn't want her upset with me!

Bunny's husband, Barry (yes, both Bunny and Heidi married men named Barry!) is a fun elf too. He likes to work the line and try to get potential screamers used to the idea of seeing Santa before the moment arrives.

One night Walt and Sue Ellsmore, who worked for me at FODAC, brought their grandson, Austin, to see Santa. He got as far as the window, looked inside, and refused to go any farther. He didn't cry, but he let them know he was not going to come in to see me.

Barry had volunteered at FODAC and knew Walt and Sue. He asked me what they were doing, standing outside. I told him that Austin didn't want to come in. He said, "Well, I can handle that." He went out, and I watched as he put his arm around the kid (they were about the same size) and whispered in his ear. In a moment they came through the door, hand in hand. Austin got right up on my lap and gave me his list, while Walt took a whole bunch of pictures. I never did find out just what Barry had said to Austin, but whatever it was, it worked and had a lasting effect. Austin was never afraid of me again.

I mentioned the yearly elf gathering at the Park on page 83, so let me tell you about the most recent one. They are always so special to me—and to the visitors who are lucky enough to see them. There are always a bunch of little people, elves and their children, all over the Park. The Johnston family invites some of their friends to come too. Last year a couple brought their daughter. This little girl is not just a little person; she is a *very* little person. She is around five but is only about the size of an eighteen-month-old. She is

More Pages from the Red Suit Diaries

a beautiful child, but tiny. Running to me as though I were her grandpa, she jumped up onto my stool, then my lap, and she talked to me like a grown-up. She knew exactly what she wanted, including brand names and model numbers. She was such a delight that I didn't want her to get down. Lucky for me, she came back later to ask some more questions and supply some additional information about her Christmas list.

## Being Santa Claus

Playing Santa Claus has given me many moments of sheer joy. And by far the most fun and satisfaction have come when I am able to be Santa to kids and grown-ups alike.

For years I had heard preachers talk about how God has a plan for your life and how you have to work at finding what his plan and purpose are for you. I never could have dreamed that one day my purpose would become so completely clear to me.

In January 1979 a young man with cerebral palsy began attending the church where I was a member. Over the next two years we had a nodding acquaintance. I knew his first name, but feeling like a coward, I tried to avoid direct eye contact with him. Looking him in the eyes would necessitate speaking, but what do you say to someone in a wheelchair? What do you say to a person whose body is twisted and racked with spasms? What in the world do you *say*?

Then over a couple of months, we began to sit and talk. I found that he was a bright, well-read man and an interesting conversationalist. I was embarrassed that for so long I had avoided getting to know him. One Sunday in February 1981 I visited him in his apartment. He lived in a complex near the church. It was called Columbia Place Apartments and had been built for wheelchair users. Over the next few months I visited him often, and one time I put a new light bulb in the light fixture over his bathroom sink.

I was shocked to discover that the simple process of replacing a light bulb gave me a feeling of accomplishment and satisfaction I had never experienced, even when I had won awards for marksmanship, sales, and writing. Those were individual accomplishments; there was something different about helping another person do something he couldn't do for himself.

On my next visit I changed a light bulb for another person in the same complex. Soon I was changing light bulbs throughout Columbia Place, and then I started doing other small chores. My building skills were being put to use.

The more I did, the more that joyful feeling swept over me. It wasn't too long before I was going through the apartment complex looking for ways to be helpful. I spent hours talking with people who had all kinds of disabilities and began to learn about the problems they faced and how they dealt with them. I began to learn that people with physical limitations are just like everyone else. They have the same hopes and dreams we all do, and their disability may or may not impede their progress toward their goals. I learned that some people collapse completely when struck by a disabling injury or illness. Others seem to be energized to overcome.

One of the biggest problems faced by wheelchair-dependent people is getting around in a world not made for wheelchairs. The simplest things, like shopping or running errands, can be a tremendous challenge. While on a sales call in Athens, Georgia, I drove by a Dodge dealership. On a whim I pulled into the used car lot. I told the salesman I was looking for a van to transport folks in wheelchairs, and he took me to the back of the lot where a retired Head Start school bus was sitting. It was a faded yellow bus with black spray paint covering the lettering on the sides, front, and rear. It looked awful, but I was more interested in how it ran and what it cost.

The salesman took me back to the offices, where he talked privately with the used car sales manager. In a few minutes he came back and told me the van was for sale for $1,200, but we could have it for $400.

"Sold!" I said.

The church I was attending paid for a folding ramp and four wheelchair tie-downs that were installed in the bus, and I began hauling folks around. We went to shopping centers, restaurants, concerts, and special events.

There were big changes going on in my life during these years. I was divorced, then met and married Annie. But my involvement with the people with disabilities was a constant that I knew was evolving and would become an even bigger part of my life.

At this point I was fully employed as a salesman of medical diagnostic equipment and supplies, covering Georgia and Alabama, as well as large portions of Tennessee and South Carolina. With all this ministry activity going on, I wasn't spending as much time on the road as I should have, but in spite of that, my sales volume continued to climb. I began to have the feeling that someone up there was definitely looking out for me. I was beginning to sense God's powerful presence and his incredible peace within my soul.

A young lady named Ann Searcy started coming to Monday night Bible study sessions that Annie and I hosted at Columbia Place and our home. After she had attended for a while, she invited her uncle, Dan Barnes, and his wife, Mary, to attend one night. They were delightful folks who seemed quite taken to be included in a roomful of people with wheelchairs or other mobility aids. After the session, they asked a lot of questions and told us they were members of Mount Carmel Christian Church in Decatur. Mr. and Mrs. Barnes said they were going to speak to the senior minister about what we were doing.

I knew a little about Mount Carmel Christian Church. The baccalaureate services for three of my children's high school graduations had been held there. On those occasions I had been impressed with the senior pastor, Jack Ballard. Jack had been the pastor for more than thirty years, and he had built the church into the largest congregation in that part of the county. Mount Carmel performed the Living Christmas Tree program each year, and we had taken our old bus, loaded with disabled folks, to enjoy it for the last five years. It was a wonderful, highly professional performance.

In a few days Dan called to say that he had spoken to his Kiwanis Club of South DeKalb, and they wanted to give us $500. But there was a wrinkle. They couldn't just give the money to Ed and Annie; they had to give it to an organization.

Annie and I spent a couple of weeks trying to decide on a name for our ministry. We kept coming back to the fact that we were simply friends of several people with disabilities, all of whom were adults. We considered several alternatives and finally settled on calling our efforts Friends of Disabled Adults, Inc.—FODA for short. (Later we began ministering to children as well, and in 1996 we changed our name to Friends of Disabled Adults and Children.)

We hired an attorney I knew to file the incorporation documents. The Kiwanis Club didn't wait for the paperwork; they sent the check as soon as we told them our name. We used that check to open the FODA checking account. We also called the IRS and had them send us the packet of papers to file for 501(c)(3) status and had the attorney draw up a set of bylaws for us. This process would take over a year, and several refilings, before we were granted permanent IRS nonprofit status. The document was dated November 10, 1987. Funny, I had celebrated that date as the birthday of the Marine Corps for more than twenty years, and now it was a birthday of sorts of our new endeavor.

As we pondered all of this, we had a phone call from Jack Ballard at Mount Carmel. Dan and Mary Barnes had told him about our Bible study and the things we were doing, and he asked us to come to his office the following Monday. I have to admit it was exciting to wonder just what might come of our visit.

The meeting began with Jack telling us of all the ways Mount Carmel had been involved in ministering to people with disabilities over the years. Jack's own secretary was a polio survivor. He had visited her in the hospital right after she was diagnosed at age eighteen. He promised her a job then, and he had kept his promise. She would hold that job for thirty-eight years.

Jack had helped a man named Jim Pierson realize his dream of a home for people with mental disabilities where they would be treated with Christian love and given the opportunity to become all that they could be. Mount Carmel's Church Builders program built the facility in Tennessee where that dream became a reality.

We told Jack about our work with the people we knew and invited him to visit the apartment complex where they lived. He said he would like to get Jim Pierson to come from Tennessee and go with him to get another perspective. When we left, he said he would call Jim and be in touch with us.

On the ride home we calculated that it would be at least a couple of weeks before they'd be able to schedule a visit. But when we got home, there was a message on our answering machine from Jack. Jim would be in town on Thursday. Clearly Jack was a person who made things happen. We would soon learn just how true that was.

On Thursday we met at Mount Carmel and all four of us went to the apartment complex in my company car. We toured the place and showed them all the little repair jobs I had done. Those two grown men stood in the middle of the courtyard and cried real tears as they saw the size of the need we had tried to fill. They understood how essential our undertaking was, even more than we did.

When we arrived back at Mount Carmel, Jack said, "I'm going to talk to our missions committee and see if we can't add you to our missions program and get you some financial support."

Annie and I couldn't help but wonder how much support it would be. We figured it would take a while to hold a committee meeting, bring it up, discuss it, and get a vote on it. We thought that some of the committee members would want to see our work for themselves.

We got home and were astounded to find that there was a message from Jack. He had already gotten the approval from the missions committee to support us—starting on the next mission Sunday. The amount of that support would be a $1,000 per month. Years later I found out that the moment he got back to his office, he set up a conference call with all the members of the missions committee, made a presentation about our project, and called for a vote on supporting us. The vote was unanimous.

We collapsed on the sofa with tears of joy, shock, and thanksgiving. We had been doing our thing for more than five years, and we had had a total of $400-worth of help, including $250 for the as-yet-unmodified van sitting in our driveway. Here was the money to make our ministry really viable.

Just a week before this we had bought the van. And look what had happened already! To Annie it was a matter of fact—acknowledgment that God had kept his promise to take care of all of us if we ask. To me it was an awesome lesson in trust, taught to me by my sweetie and a loving God. It was a lesson that was hammered into my hard head again and again before I reached the point, where Annie already was, that I could simply step out in faith *knowing* that God would honor my trust.

We also reconsidered the series of "coincidences" that had brought us to this point. Impossible things had happened too many times for there not to have been a Power greater than us working them out. Clearly this Power had plans for us that were bigger than we were. The song "Awesome God" became an anthem for us.

The miracles continued, and soon it would become apparent that God had a plan for us. I felt like I was barreling down a beautiful highway in a Rolls Royce without a steering wheel. I didn't know where we were headed, but I did know we were getting there in a style I could never have imagined.

❧

Early on, I asked Jack what the process was for ordination in his church. He suggested that I attend Atlanta Christian College and learn more about the church and the fellowship it belonged to. I called the college, met with the dean of men, and was enrolled for the term starting in January 1987.

I was still working full-time, so I signed up for one evening class and two classes that met all day one Monday a month. I was required to call my regional manager every Monday at nine. Occasionally he asked me to meet him for lunch on that day. Classes began at 8 a.m., but my teacher agreed to let me out of class for the few minutes it took to make the call. My boss never once asked me to meet him on my class days, but he did ask me three times on the Mondays when I did not have class. My heart was stirred with the undeniable truth that someone else was taking care of my schedule. God himself was directing my path.

Taking college courses was an arduous undertaking, but I set my mind to it and pressed on. About a year later we decided that it was time to quit my overpaid job as a salesman and start helping folks full-time.

Later that fall Annie and I were having dinner in a Chinese restaurant when I noticed a woman staring at me. I had never been checked out so shamelessly in my life. I began to wonder what she was seeing, and

I checked to make sure I was properly buttoned and zipped. When she and her friend finished their meal, they came to our table and asked if I was a professional Santa Claus. I told her no but that I would like to be. She handed me a card and told me to call her. This new venture would not only provide a wonderful element of fun and love in our lives, but would be a big help financially as well.

But—slow learner that I am—I still did not make a connection between the ministry and Santa. It wouldn't be until the middle of my first season as a mall Santa that I would realize there was no coincidence about this converging of tasks.

Here's why. When we started, the one thing we were sure we wanted to do was provide transportation for folks. Four days after we started full-time, I had a call from one of our folks telling me there was a wheelchair by the dumpster at Columbia Place Apartments if I wanted it. I figured I could fix it up and give it to someone who needed it, so I went and got it. That simple act put us on the path of what would become the most important thing our ministry would accomplish. Over the next twenty years we would find, collect, refurbish, and give away more than twenty thousand wheelchairs—manuals of all kinds, electrics, and scooters. It didn't take long before newspapers began to call, and in 1992 *NBC Nightly News* ran a piece about what this Santa was doing in his real workshop. When he introduced the piece, Tom Brokaw referred to me as "the real thing." From then on I was known as the Wheelchair Santa.

## Kimberly

We started out providing services to adults, but it soon became apparent that God was sending us children who needed help as well. When I was looking for parts for the first five wheelchairs, I connected with a small company in Tucker owned by Joe and Kathy Mc-Gehee, a delightful couple. They must have thought I was crazy when I told them what we intended to do.

But they did get the parts for me—and sold them to us at a better-than-retail price.

A few months later Kathy called me and said they had twenty-four children's wheelchairs that they would give us. We had never intended to do children's chairs, but this was an offer I couldn't refuse. I told Kathy we would take the chairs, and when I hung up the phone, I said out loud, "I guess the Lord wants us to do chairs for children."

After we got the twenty-four chairs, one of our first calls was from the family of four-year-old Kimberly. A stroke had caused her to lose her ability to speak and to walk, and she suffered from spasms so that she simply could not sit still. The family had cleared their living room and furnished it with mattresses. Kimberly's parents had a cheesecake business in the basement of their house, and one of them had to be upstairs to watch Kimberly all the time. They were hoping that being strapped in a wheelchair would enable her to sit still at least part of the time.

They brought Kimberly to my house for an assessment. She was a beautiful little lady, but her spasms were awful. I was not at all sure that a wheelchair would help control her involuntary movements.

I picked out a chair, cleaned it up, set up the positioning pads and straps, and called the family back. I placed Kimberly in the chair and fastened the seatbelt. She was still having spasms. I put a butterfly brace across her chest, but her legs and arms continued to flail. I put the knee separator in place, pulled her feet into position on the footrests, and strapped them down.

Kimberly took a deep breath, raised her head up to look at the TV on the shelf over the workbench, gave a long sigh, put her hands in her lap, and sat perfectly still. Her mom and dad grabbed each other and started to cry. Between sobs, her mother said, "That is the first time she's sat still while awake in over a year."

Nobody was more surprised than I was. I said out loud, "Thank you, Lord."

Mom responded, "Yes, praise the Lord. And thank you too, Santa."

Kimberly improved over the years and was able to attend public school. In more recent years, I have lost track of her, but my hope is that her life has been filled with calm and quiet moments.

## Jacob

A special group of ladies made this next Santa encounter so very special. Kim was with the Fraternal Order of Eagles Ladies Auxiliary in Doraville, Georgia. The group was raising money to buy a wheelchair for a little guy named Jacob. He was only eight years old and had severe cerebral palsy. He had two wishes: to get an electric wheelchair and to go to Disney World. His therapists had agreed that Jacob's spasms would keep him from being able to operate an electric wheelchair. But his parents felt he was more coordinated than that. The auxiliary had decided to raise the money, get the chair, and see how Jacob could handle it.

They were making some progress toward their goal of $6,400 when Kim called FODAC to see if we would make a donation to their wheelchair fund. When she learned that we would *give* Jacob a wheelchair, Kim couldn't believe it.

We had a virtually new chair that had been sitting for a few months, waiting for the right person. It was the perfect size for Jacob. His parents brought Jacob in for a first fitting, and he was enthralled by the special room for kids we call Santa's office. When the door is opened, all kinds of things begin to happen. The lights on the Christmas tree and around the room come on. Several animated characters begin to move. Christmas music plays and an animated Santa sings out, "A Holly Jolly Christmas." Two electric trains begin to chug—one around a track just above the door, and the other at the base of the tree. My gold throne spends most of the year there. A huge, stuffed Mickey Mouse keeps it warm.

We decided to have Santa there to make the delivery. As it just so happened, this would be the ten-thousandth wheelchair we would give away. I made sure I would be there when it happened.

Jacob brought an entourage with him. His mom and dad, his grandmother, and several of the Eagles ladies came to see Jacob receive his new chair. We also had two television crews there to record the event. It was quite a moment. Within a few minutes, after brief instructions from Bruce Williams, our volunteer electric shop manager and wheelchair user himself, Jacob took the controls and drove himself across the room. The crowd burst into applause. This was the very first time Jacob had controlled his own movements anywhere. There were no dry eyes in the place. Even Vernon Jones, the DeKalb County CEO, had tears on his cheeks. Bruce asked Jacob if he liked the chair, and Jacob nodded. Then Bruce asked if he was happy. And Jacob whispered, "Yes."

After a hug from Santa, Jacob was anxious to get outside and on with the rest of his life, so we stood in the lobby and watched him go. His mother came to me and threw her arms around my neck, then worked her way down the chain of command, hugging everybody in sight. Finally she managed to squeak out a "thank you" as she followed her son out the door.

This wasn't the last time we saw Jacob, as he would stop in occasionally to thank us again. At the next year's Walk and Roll fundraiser, he won the prize for raising the most money of all the several hundred attendees. His just being there driving his wheelchair was the best part. It was a brand-new chair, paid for by his dad's insurance plan. Once the therapists saw that he could handle driving the electric chair, they approved his request for one. He was riding in high style now but was still using the chair FODAC gave him when he was at school.

## Rachel

One of our most defining and joyful Santa moments came with a child we would never actually meet.

I was sitting at my desk at FODAC when a call came in from a soldier at Fort Riley, Kansas. His name was

George and he was helping a local group raise money for a wheelchair for three-year-old Rachel. She had cerebral palsy, but it had affected only her legs. She could not support her weight or walk, but the rest of her body was fine. Her father was a farmer and times were tough, as they were for many small farmers. It looked like they were about to lose their farm and they could not afford health insurance.

George had helped out at a barbecue dinner the previous Saturday. It had been a cold, rainy day, and they had managed to raise only $400 toward their goal of $7,000.

George was telling me all this as a preamble to asking us for money for a chair for Rachel. I interrupted to tell him that we didn't have any money we could contribute, but that we could give Rachel an electric wheelchair, custom fitted for her. He stammered for a moment, then asked, "Do you really mean that?"

I told him that all I needed for him to do was send me some photos of Rachel sitting in a kitchen chair so I could set up the wheelchair properly, and I would find a way to get it to them absolutely free of any charges. He said he could do that—but it took some more convincing to get him to believe that it would actually happen.

As soon as I hung up the phone, I went out into the warehouse and found a very nice Invacare Jaguar. The red paint on it was in great shape. It barely looked used, although the rear tires were both flat. I pushed it into the shop and told the guys to get it ready. It was going to Kansas.

On the same day that Rachel's pictures arrived, the shop guys brought me the chair. It looked terrific—cleaned, polished, and with solid inserts in the tires so they would never go flat again. I adjusted the footrests according to the photos. I sat on the armrests, giving it the torture test. I even drove it around for a while myself. It worked perfectly.

Bob McMullen, one of our volunteers, took a donated pallet and cut it in half. He strapped the chair onto it, used some donated plywood to build a crate around it, packed the crate with stuffed animals donated by The Disney Store, nailed the top on, painted "To Rachel, from Santa" on the side of the crate, and pronounced it ready to go.

Gene Seay, one of our friends at Mount Carmel Christian Church, arranged for the chair to get a free ride to George at Fort Riley. I took our donated forklift and loaded the crate into the back of a donated Mazda pickup truck, then drove it over to the freight company near the airport. The gas had been purchased using money we received for donated aluminum cans, collected by another Mount Carmel friend and volunteer.

Four days later I had a call from George. He started off the conversation by saying, "I know why you do what you do."

"You do?"

"Yeah, I do. The feeling that I got from delivering that chair to Rachel last night has to be happening at your place all the time. You do that because of the good feeling you get every time that happens."

I told him, "Yeah, that is a good feeling. But a better one is when I know that the Lord put this deal

More Pages from the Red Suit Diaries

together, working out the details way ahead of when they were needed, and that he covered every detail of the costs."

He told me that when they opened the crate, Rachel squealed with delight at the sight of the stuffed animals. And then, when Rachel sat in the chair and put her hands on the controls, the squeals really got going. It was dark, so they went inside and Rachel went driving around, crashing into the furniture and walls, squealing all the way. Her parents, George, and the friends he had taken over there with him were all squealing too.

I told him that a woman in Appleton, Wisconsin, had sent the wheelchair to us. She had been collecting used equipment for a while when she saw a story about us on television and decided we should have it. A Kimberly-Clark Corporation truck driver had brought the stuff (free of charge) to Atlanta on one of his trips to the local office. Total expenditures for this entire venture? Zero. Nothing. Nada. Not a penny. We do serve an awesome God.

A few days later I had a call from Rachel's mother. She told me she had not been able to call earlier because she was too emotional. She told me that the morning after the chair arrived, she and Rachel went out into the yard. Rachel was driving around, still squealing, when she pulled up next to the steps where Mom was sitting.

Her eyes were big and she was so excited. "Mom!" she exclaimed, "Mom, I can feel the wind in my ears!"

Mom and I had to pause for a moment to let the lumps clear from our throats. She went on, "My little girl can't run and play like the other kids, so she never felt the wind before. For the first time in her life, she could feel the wind because of something she was doing herself, operating her wheelchair. I just want to thank you for putting the wind in my little girl's ears."

Now I really had a lump! I couldn't respond.

Mom went on, "We saved the side of the crate that says, 'To Rachel, from Santa,' and we are all going to be believers for the rest of our lives."

I managed to recover enough to thank her for the call and to tell her it would be one I would remember forever.

Several months later, I had a letter from Rachel's mom. She told me that they had lost the farm and had moved to town, where her husband had taken an industrial job. They lived on Main Street. Every day Rachel rode up to the businesses along the street and visited the many friends she had made. She had become a "real gadabout," where before she had been very shy and withdrawn. Mom sent me a picture of Rachel sitting in the chair and looking toward the camera. Her beautiful face had an impish grin and was framed by a mantle of bright red curls. What a delightful picture!

George was right. That is why I do what I do—that good feeling.

### *Anne McGrady Crooke*

Sometimes that good feeling has nothing to do with children. Relating Santa's love and God's love to these special people may require some extra effort but sometimes produces surprising rewards.

I had seen Anne Crooke occasionally around Columbia Place Apartments. Usually, she was going to get her mail. She always wore a Vanity Fair nightgown or pajamas with a Vanity Fair robe. I knew what apartment she lived in, but she had remained aloof from us and we left her alone. We exchanged pleasant greetings, but she didn't seem to want conversation. She refused offers to join our Bible study group or to participate in any of the events we set up. From other tenants, I discovered that she was a chain smoker and had a drinking problem.

Don Nelson was a friend of hers and helped her out by walking her dog and sometimes going to the store for her. Then one day Don told me that Anne wanted me to take her to the dentist.

When I arrived for the trip, she was wearing her usual nightgown and robe. It soon became clear that she didn't have any regular clothes to wear. Her dentist was near Piedmont Hospital in Atlanta. Many times over the years I took her there and also to her doctor. I got to know both of them rather well.

At one point Anne told me that her sister had died and that she was unable to get to North Carolina for the funeral. Later she said that her sister had left her an inheritance of more than $30,000. A woman she called her "maid" came in once a week or so and cleaned her apartment and went grocery shopping for her. I discovered that most of the "groceries" were in liquid form. Somehow I just knew there was something fishy about that arrangement.

Then disaster struck. Don Nelson was walking his and Anne's dogs on the sidewalk along Columbia Drive, a very busy street. The dogs were playing and nipping at each other and Anne's dog, Poochie, jumped into the street. Instantly he was hit by a passing car. Don carried the body back to Anne's apartment and laid it on her table. Anne, understandably, wept and wailed, and Don finally had to pry the body from her arms to take it out for burial. She continued her demonstrative mourning. She got her bottles out and proceeded to get completely inebriated. The next day her maid found her in that condition and, doing as she was told, went and bought more booze.

Anne told everyone that she was going to drink herself to death, and she worked hard at it. She did not leave her bed for the next two weeks, not even for a trip to the bathroom. I did not go by her apartment during that time, but I heard from Don that it was getting really awful in there. One day the woman who ran the Meals on Wheels program called me, saying that her delivery volunteers reported that Anne was in real trouble. She did not appear to be eating the meals they were delivering, and she was completely drunk every day.

A little later, Don's dad, Dick Nelson, called and told me that we were going to have to do something. I had a transport to do but said I would come over there when I was finished. I asked if he and Don could get Anne cleaned up. He promised to try. When I called back, Dick told me Anne was refusing to let them wash her. I spoke to Anne and told her that I was coming

More Pages from the Red Suit Diaries

over and that she'd better be cleaned up when I got there. I was not going to take no for an answer.

I arrived at Columbia Place as soon as possible. Several people were there, and Anne was sitting on her somewhat cleaner but still uninhabitable bed. It was awful. The several layers of blankets, sheets, and waterproof pads did not make it any better. I sat in a chair across from her, observing her completely drunken state. I said quietly, "Hey, Anne, what is going on?"

She answered in a near stupor, "My Poochie got killed, and I am going to drink myself to death."

"Well, I really don't want you to do that." I answered. "Why don't we see what your doctor has to say about it?"

"I don't care what he says," she mumbled. "I got no reason to live anymore. I just want to die."

As she was talking, I was dialing her doctor's number. To my profound shock, I reached him. After I identified myself, he said, "Well, hi, Ed. How is Ms. Crooke doing?"

I told him about the dog and that she was drunk and intended to do herself in. He said we couldn't let that happen but that he couldn't admit her for being drunk. I looked down at her feet hanging off the side of the bed and told him that her circulation problem was worse than ever, that she needed treatment soon.

He said, "Great, then she definitely needs to be in the hospital for at least three weeks. We can work together to get her in a safer place."

I told him I was bringing her to Piedmont, and he agreed to meet us in the ER. I hung up and called an ambulance service. I wasn't about to transport her in my van. I didn't think she could sit up in a wheelchair, and I didn't have a gurney.

Of course Anne had heard this conversation and was hollering that she was not going to go to "any stupid hospital," and she didn't care what I said. The other people in the room watched quietly as the drama unfolded.

While we waited for the ambulance, I took all her booze to the sink and personally poured every drop

More Pages from the Red Suit Diaries

down the drain. Everyone watched. Some offered to help, but that was one job I wanted to do myself, giving her reason to be mad at me only. Next, I went through her dresser drawers and collected her bank statement, checks, and checkbook, along with other personal records. I was concerned that in her condition, her finances and records were vulnerable.

When the ambulance came, they brought in a gurney. I motioned to Anne and said, "Take her to Piedmont ER." An EMT asked if we were related. I told her, "I am embarrassed to tell you this, but she's my mama." (Yes, it was a lie, which was later confessed and forgiven.)

Anne exploded in protestations, "I am not his mama. I don't even know him. I don't even have any children. Don't let him do this to me. I don't want to go to the hospital. Don't you dare take me to the hospital!"

Looking at the EMTs, shaking my head, I said, "She does this to me all the time. I am so embarrassed."

They nodded. Then they forced her onto the gurney and strapped her down. She went out the door, hollering all the way.

I told the people there to take her mattress and bedding out to the dumpster and to take the bed (a lovely antique spool bed) outside and hose it off. They also had to soak the floor under the bed with disinfectant.

I got to the hospital before the ambulance and went straight to the ER to talk to the doctor. When the ambulance pulled up, the crew told me she had hollered so much that she had hyperventilated. They'd had to give her oxygen during the ride. They were glad to get rid of her.

The doctor took Anne into an exam room, and I went home. A few days later I called and talked to the nurses on her floor. They begged me to come and get her out of there. I could hear her yelling in the background. I told the nurse I would come down in a few days. The doctor had promised me three weeks of hospitalization, and I was going to use all of it. During that time I cleaned out Anne's apartment and stored her furniture at FODAC. I cancelled her phone and stopped her month-to-month lease. I talked to a social worker at the hospital, asking her to find a rehabilitation/nursing home that would take Anne in directly from the hospital. Medicare would pay for a certain number of days, and I knew she needed every one of them.

I went to the hospital at the end of her second week. When I walked into her room, she looked completely different. She was stone sober, and her eyes were clear. Unfortunately, her temperament had not changed. She lit into me like a mad hornet, yelling and threatening me with several kinds of revenge. She told me she was going to go back to her apartment and take up right where she had left off.

I announced that she no longer had an apartment and that she was going into a nursing home. Now she really went berserk, with more screams, threats, and ugly words. The one thing she did not do was get violent. I smiled at her once and said, "One day you are going to thank me for this." She did not calm down, so I just left.

During this time, I went through her bank statements and cancelled checks. I also found a few grocery store receipts. I matched up the transaction dates and discovered that her "maid" had been paying for $50 to $60-worth of groceries with checks of $250 to $300. No doubt she had pocketed the difference. She had even written herself a couple of checks for $500 and signed Anne's name. I wrote all this out on a lined pad. Anne's $30,000-dollar inheritance had decreased by $18,000 in five months.

The social worker called and told me she had placed Anne in a nursing home near DeKalb Medical Center. Anne was transferred by ambulance, and I was in the business office when she arrived. Once again, I told them I was her son. I could hear her belly-aching when they came in the back door. I went out the front. I was going to let her stew in her own juices for another week or so.

I called a man I knew who owned a personal care home in Tucker. He told me that he could manage to take Anne for the $1,700 monthly income she had, although the normal rate was much more.

At the nursing home, the moment I walked in the

More Pages from the Red Suit Diaries

room, Anne took off again with the crabbing and grousing. "Get me out of here," she screamed. Pointing at her three roommates, she said, "That woman is crazy and just talks gibberish all the time, that one just sits and stares at me, and the other one cries all the time. I can't take any more of this place."

I ignored her demonstration and sat down on the bed beside her. I showed her the lined pad and explained how her maid had been ripping her off and keeping her drunk so she could steal from her. I documented every entry, and proved that she could have no doubt that what I had found was true. I told her that this amounted to felony theft. I asked her if she wanted to prosecute her maid. She pondered that for a while and then said, "No."

I said that I was going to call her maid and tell her what we had found and that if she ever showed up anywhere near Anne I would have her arrested and prosecuted.

Of course, the maid denied everything but said she would not come back.

I returned to the nursing home a few days later, and Anne had calmed down some. This time she *quietly* begged me to get her out of there. I told her about the personal care home in Tucker. She said she didn't know where Tucker was and didn't want to move so far away. But I did my best to explain that this would be good for her.

Annie went to a thrift store and bought five outfits for her. We had them cleaned and put on hangers. I went back to the nursing home and showed Anne the outfits, one at a time. She found something wrong with every one of them, until the last one. She said, "I guess I could wear *that* one."

I told her I would get a nurse to help her get ready, but she just whipped off her top and said, "Here, throw it over me." I did, in a big hurry.

She protested all the way out to Tucker. But when we pulled into the parking lot and she saw the building, her entire tone changed. "This is very nice," she whispered.

I rolled her up to the door, and as we went in, she

exclaimed in as sweet a voice as you could imagine, "Hello, everybody. My name is Anne. How are you?"

The manager had been expecting us and took us to see the room and other amenities. I told Anne that I was prepared to move her furniture into her room and that I had ordered a nice custom-made mattress for her bed. I spoke about it as if it was a done deal. She went along with it.

A few people helped me move her furniture, and we hung her pictures on the walls. I told Marilyn, the manager, that if she or anyone else got booze for Anne, I would have them fired. She knew I could do that and made sure her staff understood it too.

Anne was very happy at that place, and to spice it up some, Annie and I would take her out to eat once a week or so. She always loved those times. We took her to Mount Carmel Church sometimes too. That was another special treat.

Two years went by. One night during dinner, she suddenly said, "I hate to admit it, but you were right.

I am glad you took me out of Columbia Place. I am sure I would be dead by now and would have missed out on all this fun and the wonderful life I have now."

I just said, "You're welcome."

In time, the home was sold to new owners. I talked to them, and they agreed to keep Anne on for $1,700 a month for as long as they could. But a couple of years later, they told her they had to raise the rent. So Annie and I went looking for a new home for Anne. A staff member at Tucker also worked in another residence, and we went to see it. It was very nice, and in a week Anne was moved in. The owner of this new abode took Anne lots of places and occasionally brought her to Mount Carmel.

One Sunday night I was sitting in my regular seat at the end of a pew when I felt movement to my left. I turned and there was Anne. I jumped, feigning being frightened. I said, "Good grief, woman. That's enough to scare a man to death, sneaking up on him like that. That was a mean, rotten thing to do."

More Pages from the Red Suit Diaries

She leaned over to me and said, "Is that any way to talk to your mama?" I just about fell out of my seat. That was the first and last reference she ever made about my outrageous story all those years ago.

Anne loved hearing about all the good things going on at FODAC and all the people we were helping. She delighted in my Santa role, and I always made a couple of appearances at her personal care home. She loved it and behaved like she was my mama. She gave me a precious Santa figurine, which I keep by my bed even now.

Anne developed emphysema from all those years of smoking, and her systems slowly shut down. She died in November 2001 while my Santa season was in full swing. She had lived nine years since I took her screaming and kicking out of Columbia Place. I led her memorial service one evening at her personal care home, and several of her friends were there.

There was one sad line in her obituary: "There were no survivors."

Over the course of these twenty years, we have met many other remarkable people among the sixty thousand or so who have come to us for help. It has been a constant source of amazement how some people collapse completely at the slightest interruption in their mobility while others can take almost anything in stride and keep on going.

## John Howard Haire Jr.

John Howard Haire Jr. was the son of a former mayor pro tem of the city of Atlanta. John grew up as a person of privilege, an only child, doted on by his mother and father. As our nation's involvement in World War II loomed, John wanted to be a pilot. He enrolled in the V12 program at the University of Georgia as soon as it was established. He became a multiengine instructor pilot and flew all the multi-engine aircraft in the U.S. inventory.

His marriage to a society debutante made all the papers. When I saw pictures years later, I saw that he was an incredibly handsome figure in his uniform. His gorgeous bride was from a prominent Atlanta family.

John was discharged at the end of the war and just a few weeks later suffered a massive cerebral hemorrhage. His mother moved into his room at the VA hospital and catered to his every need. It was clear that John's life had changed forever. He could not talk, his right side was paralyzed, and the right side of his face drooped. At first, he could not swallow. He was dreadfully spastic. And he would be wheelchair-dependent for the rest of his life.

Therapy in those days was rudimentary at best, but he did learn to speak again and was able to recover some use of his arms and legs. He also learned to swallow again.

When his parents took him home, his wife was gone. A couple of months later, he was served with divorce papers, and he never saw or heard from her again.

John's dad and uncle ran a furniture store, and for years John hung around there with them. When his dad and mother died, he still kept on with his uncle. Then the uncle died, and the store was sold. John was left alone and on his own. For a while he lived in a nursing home. Then the nursing home set up Columbia Place, and John was the first resident.

When Annie and I first began to help out at Columbia Place, we would see John from time to time, making his way around. He sat on the front edge of his wheelchair seat, leaning way back, and propelled himself by "walking" with his legs. A friend, Ruth, lived with him. It was a cooperative relationship, with her doing the cooking and cleaning and John providing the finances from the modest trust fund his parents and uncle had left him. He and Ruth had met at the nursing home, and both were glad to be at Columbia Place.

Soon Ruth was taken to the hospital and died within a few days. Ruth's sons had not told John anything about her condition and did not even tell him when she died. Finally he asked a friend to call the hospital and check on her. The friend ascertained that she had died several days earlier. John had missed the funeral. He was devastated over yet another loss and the painful rejection from Ruth's family.

When we met John, we knew nothing of his background. He was a gregarious, affable guy, and we had no idea what sorrow was accumulating in his heart. We invited him to the Bible study on Monday nights, and he started coming. He had a million questions. Those questions, and their answers, provided the basis for our study for a good long time. We learned about John's history—a rich history indeed. His dad, as a city councilman, was involved in some of the exciting early growth of Atlanta. Often he had taken John along to meetings and social events. John had met many of the most interesting people in Atlanta's past.

John wanted to know how a loving God could bring such a series of disasters to his life. We did, too. But there is no easy answer to that question. Although we discussed it for months, finally we decided that we just have to accept some things on faith and leave

the greatest of these is love

the answers to God. John decided he could do that, and he professed his love for Jesus and his trust in him. Instead of, "Why me?" the question became, "Why not me?"

I was still selling in those days, and because he loved to travel, I took John along on a couple of day trips. He also loved to talk, and he never slowed down, no matter how many hours we rode. At the end of the day, I felt like I'd been shot at by a machine gun. But we both had a good time.

One night in Bible study at our house, John pulled up his shirt and showed us a large mole growing right in the middle of his chest. He said, "What about this?" A chill ran through my body. Even from across the room, I was sure it was a melanoma. I told him we were going to the VA that week.

The biopsy results were not good, and the doctors wanted John to come back for a more thorough surgical procedure. John was terrified. He asked Annie all kinds of questions. He just could not understand how they could put him to sleep and cut him without

More Pages from the Red Suit Diaries

waking him up. Annie went through the entire process with him and assured him he would not feel a thing. She went to the hospital the morning of the surgery and was there when they took John to the operating room.

When he came back, Annie heard his voice in the hall and went to him. John hollered out, "You were right! It was exactly like you said it would be." They had taken out more tissue from his chest and scraped the bone on his sternum and ribs. They put him on some chemotherapy, and John went on with life. Periodically they did follow-up tests, and it was no surprise a couple of years later when the cancer returned and had spread throughout John's body. We discussed the situation with him, and he decided he wanted to go home and be with his friends when he died.

For years John had been watching a terrible old television set, but finally I convinced him to use a little of his "rainy day" money for a new one. He was thrilled that he could now see the picture clearly.

I had done John's will and was executor of his estate. I also officiated at his funeral. There were a couple of surprises. Two of John's cousins came to the funeral and told me how close they had been to John, how they had visited him many times. I had been around for eight years and had never seen anybody come to visit John. They asked about a will, and I told them there was one, but that they were not in it. They left.

Then John's former wife showed up. She did not ask about the will. She said that she had been the one who had ordered the flowers and fruit baskets that John had found outside his door for many years. She said she stayed away because when she remarried, she married a man who had been John's best friend in high school. He had visited John many times, never telling John whom he had married. She apologized for neglecting him.

We learned a lot from John. No matter how many times he got knocked down, he always got up and kept going. He had a wonderful sense of humor and an incredible attitude. He had once been a very capable man, but even though the stroke had left his face disfigured and his body nonfunctional, he kept on going. He showed us all how to be positive and confident under the worst of circumstances.

## Hugh Ivy Harris

Another person we learned a lot from was Hugh Harris. Hugh was a lifelong smoker and had high blood pressure. At age fifty-three, he had a huge stroke. He lost the use of his right side and became aphasic—he could not get his voice to do what his mind was telling it. Before his stroke he had been an accountant in the chicken industry, and his stay-at-home wife, Elizabeth, had always waited on him hand and foot. It was only natural that she continue to do so after the stroke. They lived that way until, eleven years later, she died suddenly of a heart attack. Hugh was devastated. There was no way he could live alone. He tried living with his son Rob in Atlanta for a few weeks, but that proved to be a disastrous situation. So he went to El Paso, Texas, and lived with his daughter.

Within a few weeks, his daughter had had enough. Unable to cope with her dad's disability and constant demands, she told him she was not going to wait on him hand and foot and that he had to learn to take care of himself. He learned to make a sandwich and fix his own lunch. But he was such an irascible old coot that his daughter finally bought him a ticket back to Atlanta. Rob found him an apartment at Columbia Place and unceremoniously dumped him there with a few furniture items to help make him comfortable. But he was miserable.

Enter Ed and Annie.

Fortunately, Hugh had come to terms with his attitude and decided he had better adjust to the reality of his life if he was going to survive living alone. Hugh was suspicious of us for a long time, but bit-by-bit he came to realize that we were really there because we wanted to help. He became a regular in our group and our Monday night Bible study, and we found him to be a rather pleasant gentleman. Though he struggled to say what he wanted to say, the rest of us waited patiently—except for John, who would try to help Hugh by finishing his sentences or trying to guess what Hugh was trying to say. It made Hugh furious.

One night Hugh got so mad at John that he scooted across the room in his wheelchair with his cane raised over his head. Luckily, I was nimble and quick enough to prevent Hugh from whacking John over the head. John was not coordinated enough to defend himself. As long as John didn't interrupt, they got along all right. We had tried to get John to quit interrupting, but it took this incident to finally shut him up.

Hugh was a quieter traveling companion than John, and I took him on several of my selling trips, even some overnights. Hugh loved movies, particularly science fiction, so on overnight trips we went to movies together. We were in Dothan, Alabama, one time and he talked me into going to a movie called *The Last Starfighter*. I loved it, and it has become one of my all-time favorites. I have it on both videotape and DVD.

On one of our trips together, Hugh told me he had one regret about his life. He had never told his daughter, Mary Beth, that he loved her. I was shocked. He said he couldn't say it over the phone, and she couldn't afford to come for a visit. I tracked her down and called her, telling her that Hugh desperately wanted to talk to her and that I would pay her way to fly to Georgia.

She told me she would rather drive her car and bring her daughter with her, so I told her I would buy the gas and pay for the motel rooms coming and going. They would stay with Annie and me. A couple of weeks later she called to say she was on the way and would be here the next day. That was when I told Hugh she was coming.

The next morning I went early to fetch him. I sat Mary Beth directly in front of Hugh's wheelchair. They just stared at each other for a good while. Then I said softly, "Hugh, don't you have something you want to tell Mary Beth?"

There was a long pause while he struggled to produce the words. Then he suddenly blurted out, "I love you!"

Mary Beth sat stunned for a moment, then lunged for her dad and hugged him. When she quit sobbing, she said, "I have waited all my life to hear you say that. Why did you never tell me that before?"

Hugh struggled to answer and finally said, "I wanted to. I wanted to. I wanted to. I just couldn't. I'm sorry. So sorry. So sorry."

She moved closer to Hugh and took his good hand. She leaned forward and placed his hand on her cheek. "I love you too, Daddy. I love you too."

I left the room and let them share their feelings for as long as they wanted. When we went to lunch, they continued their sharing. Then we went back to the house, and they talked until Hugh said that he had to go home.

They spent the next three days together. They visited Rob and went to Rome, Taylorsville, Cedartown, and other places to see relatives and Elizabeth's grave.

Each night Mary Beth reported to me what they had done and thanked me for making it happen. When she finally had to leave, she said that Hugh had told her he loved her over and over again during those days.

Refusing my offer to pay for the trip, she said it was the best investment she had ever made. She hugged Annie and me, and she and her daughter drove away. It had been a wonderful time for us too, and it had a magical effect on Hugh. He was no longer the grumpy old man he had once been.

Soon after that visit, Hugh developed leukemia and began to require periodic blood transfusions. At first, it was every couple of months, then monthly, then twice a month, then weekly. I took him for every session. I knew that his days were numbered by his willingness to continue the needle sticks and transfusions. The nurses at DeKalb Medical Center were wonderful, and Hugh became one of their favorites.

Hugh had an enormously concerned doctor who, at one point, put him into the hospital for a complete evaluation, telling me that Hugh was about to run out

More Pages from the Red Suit Diaries

of options. I contacted Hugh's son, who had visited his dad frequently.

Finally, Hugh told me that he didn't want any more transfusions. He had already had more than a hundred. He repeated over and over, "No more, no more, no more."

I called the nurse, requesting a visit from Hugh's doctor. As we waited, Hugh and I talked about all the fun we had had together, and he reminded me of the time we saw *The Last Starfighter*. We had a wonderful time reminiscing. When the doctor got there, he went over the medical implications of Hugh's decision. Hugh let him know he fully understood that without another transfusion, he could live only a few days. He repeated, "Ready to go, ready to go, ready to go, ready to go." His mind was made up.

The next morning, when Annie and I got to his room, he said, "Elizabeth," and pointed to a corner of the room.

I said, "Are you telling me Elizabeth is over there?"

He nodded emphatically.

I said, "She has come for you, Hugh."

"Yeah," he answered, then repeated, "Ready to go, ready to go, ready to go."

I had talked to Rob the previous night, and he told me he was coming that afternoon. Annie and I left just before noon. It was clear that Hugh was fading.

At dusk a nurse called to tell us that Hugh had just died. Rob had been there and left about thirty minutes earlier. We told her we were on our way. Hugh looked more peaceful than we had seen him since Mary Beth left four years earlier.

The nurse told us that Hugh had called her into his room and motioned for her to sit beside him on the bed. She did and put her arm around Hugh's shoulders. He was breathing short, gasping breaths, which she recognized as his final ones. Then suddenly he sat up, looked straight into the corner of the room, and almost shouted, "Elizabeth!" Then a big smile spread over his face, and he lay back on the bed and took his final breath.

More Pages from the Red Suit Diaries

Hugh had chosen the time and place for his death and had been greeted by the one true love of his life. What a way to go!

I presided at Hugh's funeral. We drove him the seventy miles to Cedartown, where he and Elizabeth had lived. Rob and other relatives gathered at the cemetery and we had a commitment service, laying him beside his beloved Elizabeth. Hugh was home.

## Teresa, Chris, and Rita

Early in our ministry we had taken a group of our friends to South DeKalb Mall. As we were loading up to take them home, a woman who was passing by asked me if we were a transportation service for people in wheelchairs. I told her about our ministry, and she asked me what it cost to make a trip. I told her it was all absolutely free. She told me she had a friend with multiple sclerosis who lived in her apartment building and needed rides to different places. I gave her a card and told her to have her friend call me.

A few days later I had a call from a woman whose Bronx accent immediately enchanted me. She told me about her life with MS and asked if I could take her to the dentist the following week. I said that I could, and you would have thought I had promised her a ride to heaven. She told me she had a brother and sister who were both developmentally disabled, and they would go along but that they did not require much supervision.

When I arrived for the pickup, they were waiting outside the building. Finally I understood her name as Teresa Rienzie. She introduced her brother, Chris, and her sister, Rita. They mumbled a response, and then Teresa told me that the two of them had a language all their own and did not talk much in plain English. I had heard of that phenomenon before. Though they couldn't read, write, or tell time, they actually communicated extremely well with each other.

When we got to the dental office, I pushed Teresa into the waiting room. Chris and Rita sat next to her, and I sat across the room. When the dental tech came for Teresa, Chris and Rita got up immediately and sat next to me. I was reading a magazine. They mimicked my movements, thumbing through the pages, looking at the pictures.

The moment Teresa came back, they both moved to be near her. Chris took the push handles of her chair, and Rita stood beside her. They were protecting her.

Teresa told me they were from a family of twelve children. Chris and Rita were the youngest. There was another sister, Mary, who lived in Augusta, Georgia, and was available when they needed her. Teresa was my age and was an Air Force veteran. Chris and Rita were two and four years younger.

Over the years I took them many places. We went to doctors, dentists, drug stores, and grocery stores. I came to have a profound respect for all of them. This was an amazing relationship. Teresa needed help with her physical needs as MS slowly destroyed her body. Chris and Rita needed someone to help with their mental needs. It was a perfect synergistic relationship. Teresa would sit in the doorway of the kitchen and instruct Chris and Rita as they prepared the meals. They got Teresa out of bed every morning, gave her a shower, brushed her teeth, dressed her, and put her in her electric recliner chair. They did all the laundry and cleaned the house. Teresa had a schedule for every task and supervised every step.

Chris and Rita always called me Santa Claus, and a couple of times I wore my full Red Suit out to their house. I took each of them a cuddly stuffed teddy bear. They loved the whole experience.

They bought a house and lived together until the MS had run its course and Teresa died. Mary told me that when she shared the news with Chris and Rita, they stood and stared at her for a few minutes. Then Chris said, "Well, that is over." The two of them sat down on the couch to watch TV. They did not mention Teresa again.

There was no service. Teresa was cremated, and

her ashes were to be scattered when they went back to New York someday.

It was an amazing story of how family members should stick together and take care of each other. That doesn't always happen. In this case it did in an amazing way.

# *final miracles*

## Final Miracles

When all these "little" miracles have been added up, it amounts to some bigger, rather significant ones.

We began FODAC in my garage, and now we are in a 64,885-square-foot building. It was quite a process that got us here, but seeing it is still a shock for all of us at FODAC and for our visitors. Every time I pull into the parking lot, I still can't believe all this has happened to us.

Inside, the forty-thousand-square-foot warehouse is crammed with medical equipment of all kinds, shapes, sizes, and descriptions. We have thousands of parts and hundreds of devices. There are shelves and pallet racks everywhere. The parts themselves are worth millions of dollars. They haven't cost FODAC a single cent. The offices and shop spaces are filled with desks, computers, chairs, and artwork on the walls. Some spaces even have fancy lighting. And it all came to us as donations. We have a sixteen-foot-long conference table in our boardroom—a donation. I can't walk through our building without thinking all the time, *What an awesome God we serve*!

Consider the effects that all these miracles have had. We gave away our ten thousandth wheelchair in December 2003. We are over twenty thousand now. We have provided wheelchairs to people in forty-two states and in sixty-eight countries. Those numbers are mind-boggling. We started out to help the twelve people we were already connected to, and now more than sixty thousand people have benefited from our obedience to our loving Lord.

We have an area in our office space where we have put up thank-you notes on the wall. There are hundreds of them. Anytime the staff or I need a boost, we can recharge our batteries by reading some of these letters. Just walking by them gives me all the charge I need.

More Pages from the Red Suit Diaries

Our ramps program has built more than seven hundred ramps all over north Georgia. Every one of them represents an entire family whose lives are made just a little bit easier. People are able to go to church, to the store, and to medical appointments again with minimal assistance.

Hundreds more people have found affordable clothing in our thrift store. We have given clothing and furniture to families who have lost their homes and clothing to homeless people who are going for job interviews. We have given shelters refrigerators and freezers and mattresses—literally, tons of them.

We've been able to provide people with vehicles. We have enabled several people with disabilities to go to college. We have made it possible for families that were completely homebound to get out and enjoy life again. Is it any wonder that people call me Santa Claus?

It has been a remarkable adventure, this trip. We have never once doubted that we were doing the exact thing that God wanted us to do. Of course, there has been some anxiety from time to time, when things didn't happen when or how we thought they should. But we have come to realize that God's timetable is different from ours. He has come through on his schedule, which usually works out better than ours would have anyway.

I found out at the age of fifty that God was waiting for me to yield to him, and then he went right to work making things happen. Our God is a gentleman; he never forces himself on anyone. He is available to you too. If you haven't already, why don't you invite him to take control of your life and find out what special joy he can bring to your heart?

That good feeling doesn't require a red suit and a white beard. It does require wearing Christ's love right out there where people can see and feel it. It does require being kind and loving in all your dealings with everyone. Yes, even the clerks in stores, tellers in the bank, service writers at the auto repair shop, and everyone else you encounter. Put a smile on your

More Pages from the Red Suit Diaries

face and see how many smiles you will see in return. Smiling is contagious—pass it around!

Jesus gave us two commands: love God and love your neighbors. It's simple, really. Show your love for God by loving your neighbors. Find a way to do that. Reach out to others in love. Volunteer at a service charity. Build a Habitat house. Give blood. Mow your neighbor's lawn. Be the type of person you'd like to be.

Be somebody's Santa Claus.

Officially Santa at Stone Mountain Park for eighteen years, **Ed Butchart** founded Friends of Disabled Adults and Children (FODAC) and operated it for twenty years until he turned over the operations to a younger man in 2005. He began in the garage of his home and turned over a 64,885-square-foot workshop to his successor. He directed a full-time staff of seventeen plus forty volunteers in repairing wheelchairs and other medical equipment for the needy. They have refurbished and provided life-changing equipment for more than sixty thousand people with disabilities in sixty-eight countries and forty-five states.

His public service and personal work have brought Butchart numerous humanitarian awards, including the Governor of Georgia and Mayor of Atlanta Commendations in 1993, the Dekalb College MLK Jr. Humanitarian Award in 1998, and the Metro Atlanta Council for Exceptional Children "Outstanding Individual" Award in 1998.

Butchart, an ordained minister, has served as an elder in his church, Mount Carmel Christian Church, and until 2007 lived in Stone Mountain, Georgia. He now lives in Greenville, South Carolina. He has five adult children.